Were Oz:

Fantasy Travel by Google Maps

Can a werewolf Halfling survive Oz and return home to its other half for a laugh?

by Dr. Marc Latham

A Greenygrey Publication

DISCLAIMER

This book is a work of fictional parody. While it features real people and places, they are taken out of their real context and transported to the fantasy world of Oz via Google maps for this exploratory expedition into comedy fantasy – magic realism virtual travelling. Only the author has had anything to do with the creation of this book. Apologies to people and places that do not think they are portrayed positively, but it is obviously fictional, and hopefully this book will create further interest in them.

The book is written from an agnostic viewpoint. Some of the material may offend religious extremists, so they are advised not to read any further. The book also contains sections involving alcoholic beverages: good times are balanced with bad.

One of the reasons the writer chose Australia; the main one is of course that its nickname, Oz, ties in with the Wizard of Oz; for this journey was because he thought Australians would appreciate the humour. It was written with fondness and respect for Australia; a country where the author spent most of 1989.

The book consciously provides a positive anthropomorphic view of animals, and especially the wolf. It is hoped that, in some small way, this might help the remaining wild animals in the world survive a little longer by raising awareness. Despite providing us with our 'best friend' dog, the wolf has suffered a particularly negative image in human cultures alienated from the wilderness. This has resulted in the wolf's persecution and extinction in many regions of the world.

Y is the 3-D tree of growth, thought and knowledge at the
heart of the
greenYgrey

Dedicated to the Munchkin Cat-aliced

PREFACE

The book was made possible by using technology that has
emerged in the digital age. Companies providing the
broadband, software and websites include: Virgin, Amazon,
Google, Wordpress, Wikipedia, Photo Impact, Microsoft,
Facebook and Koalanet (Aussie slang words). The author was
grateful to acquire friends, readers, inspiration and
information through the social media on some of those
websites. Family and friends in the real world are also
appreciated. Thanks also to those who have published,
bought and praised the author's previous work.

Writing Magazine provided most of the creative writing
advice and instruction learnt before and during the writing
of this book. The writer learnt most of his old rock from
Kerrang and *Classic Rock* magazines, and usually listened to
Planet Rock radio while working on the book. Comedy was

learnt from cartoons, comics, television, magazines, films, books, people and animals from the 1960s to the present.

Dr. Marc Latham has been editing for seventeen years: eleven years of further education and six years of creative writing. He took a six-month career break to finish the book. Researching the book was both an enjoyable form of escapism and an informative geography lesson; the author was often sent on a trip down memory lane, and maybe that's what the dust sandy path (yellow brick road) is all about.

Let this be my epic
although I am sceptic
my mind I tried to raise
hoping for literary praise
I let the cats out of the bag
so the dogs' tails would wag
I hope I wasn't howling upon
the wrong tree of life moonsun
silverlining and goldlining barks
echoing experience of funny larks
meeting people in places across Oz
Y? A fantasy quest created my cause.

1. PROLOGUE

Welcome everybody. It's Grey Werewolf here. Regular
readers of the Greenygrey will know me by now. For those
who don't, to cut a neverending story short, I'm one half of a
legendary vegetarian werewolf. Green and I are the last of
our Greenygrey kind as far as we know. We emerged into the
human world while blogging our epic ramble across North
America; before becoming Britain's most celebritious
werewolf. We are virtually legends in our own lifetime(s),
which we think is (are) many centuries long.
We were divided after an evil force took over the Greenygrey
world; Green was imprisoned and I was exiled to Oz.

Whizzing Earth's space
I did race;
like *Doctor Who's Tardis*,
through the northern
constellation of Camelopardus.

I think I passed through Cassiopeia
but to tell you the truth, it was all a blur;
it could well have been Andromeda.

Drifting through Ursa Major or Ursa Minor
I lost sight of the Great Wall of China
I recognised the three stars of Triangulum,
and felt a sense of equatorial equilibrium.

But then I saw another triangle
spinning my mind at an angle;
I asked 'Dog Star' Sirius
if it was aware of this?
It barked the name Triangulum Australe
adding I was now in the opposite locale.

When I saw the Southern Cross
I was no longer at a loss
I had read about constellation Crux
in some astronomical books.

I felt more at home in Chamaeleon
remembering my ability to chameleon
Norma was a lass, Hydrus a gas,
Mensa was a tester, Circinus a jester.

Into the atmosphere I whirled east to west
over the land of my looming test
I could make out the Great Barrier Reef
providing a valuable landmark brief
A long way from home I heard hound sound
whirled upside down I descended to ground.

It felt strange to be so far away from my Green other half,
and I sure missed that limey lobo. Even though I didn't
choose my exile, I still hoped to enjoy myself and learn from
my experiences, before one day being reunited with Green.

It turned out that I travelled to every state and territory in Oz; known to you as Australia; as Green and I did across North America. It was again quite an adventure. I met many famous people and creative products, and this time the story all came together in the end like pure fiction; unlike our American ramble, which read more like literary nonsense held together by acronyms until the very end.

I blogged the whole trip, and the chapters of this book are structured in line with the blogs. This prologue was the first of 142 blogs.

So, without further ado, and for you to view, here is my epic Ozyssey all edited for easy reading. It starts right at the beginning, when I landed all alone in the south of Western Australia.

Notes

Camelopardus, Cassiopeia, Andromeda, Ursa Major, Ursa Minor and Triangulum are all northern sky constellations. Triangulum Australe, Crux, Chamaeleon, Norma, Hydrus, Mensa and Circinus are all southern sky constellations. *Doctor Who* is a television series featuring a time-traveller. The time machine in the series is called a *Tardis*.

----

2. ARRIVAL AND RAMBLE

Alone in a new land down under, old world turned upside down.

The mounting sound of dogs barking made me think that Mount Barker would be as good a place as any to land. I wouldn't say it was a perfect landing, but it had been a long journey, and I am new to this solo space flight malarkey. A last minute shapeshift into a Swedish vallhund – schnauzer – shih tzu cross on the approach didn't help matters either. I was delighted to find that a cacophonous crowd of canines had turned out to greet me; it was cool to have charming company again. A diligent dingo called Digger told me Sirius had told them I was on my way. They had also prepared a fantastic feast, and all the anxiety I had felt on the journey quickly receded.

Digger and Aussie

I had itchy paws after the food. Although I was sorry to be leaving so soon, I thought I should get rambling, as the sooner you start the sooner you should finish. I told Digger, and it announced my departure to the crowd. They all wished me a safe journey, and I thanked them for their hospitality. I hoped everywhere would be so easy; while I didn't think it would be, I never imagined how difficult and dangerous it would become.

Digger escorted me out of town, and showed me the road to Denmark. It was a nice relaxing journey, and I reached there a few hours later. It was a nice liberal place to relax. I met an Australian Shepherd dog called Aussie there, and it gave me a guide for Australia's South West after showing me around town.

Aussie accompanied me to Greens Pool, and on the way told me it had arrived from overseas as well. It wasn't a natural Australian, but is now known as an Aussie. While Aussie was great company, Greens Pool of course brought back memories of pool swims with my dear ol' other half, Green.

Wombat of Walpole

It was already late afternoon when I bade Aussie farewell and set off north-west. It was a lovely ramble through 400-year-old red and yellow tingle trees on the way to Walpole.

I fancied a shapeshift along the way, so I changed into an Australian animal; my choice turned out to be quite fortunate, because after arriving in Walpole I made the acquaintance of a very distinguished old Wombat. And guess what animal I'd shapeshifted into?

Yes, if you guessed wombat you'd be right.

My wombat friend introduced itself as Vombatus Ursinus, but said I could call it Vombat; it was a local dignitary, and arranged for me to stay at the best burrow in town. We feasted on burritos in the dining room that night, and drank burdock and dandelion. We talked about our lives thus far, and had a lot in common for creatures from such different worlds. It was a highly enjoyable evening, but that of course meant that time flew, and it was soon time to say goodnight. Vombat said he'd arrange for me to have breakfast in burrow the next morning: a refried-beans burrito.

I thought about the wonders of travel before dropping off to sleep. I'd started the day reluctant to leave Green, and unsure of what lay ahead, but I'd had a *Fantastic Mr. Fox* time, and met some wonderful new friends along the way.

Notes

Sir Robert Walpole (Britain's first Prime-Minister).
Fantastic Mr. Fox (cartoon film).

----

3. MARGARET RIVERS IN MARGARET RIVER

Vombat sent me off with a bombastic brekkie, and I started my second day on the road in high spirits. It didn't last long; but that's not to say the day went downhill. It's just that the sea looked so serene I jumped in and shapeshifted into a whale shark to swim up the coast; so I didn't spend much time on the road. The new shape took a little getting used to, and I was flapping around on the surface for a while, looking more wombat than whale.

Whale of a Time with Whale Sharks

I met a genus of whale sharks in deep water. Winona, Walter, Wendy, William and Dweezil made me feel right at home; Dweezil seemed different to the others for some reason, but was especially funny in an oddball way. They swam quite slowly, but the relaxed pace meant I could see more of the coral and fish.
We reached Margaret River by tea-time, and after changing into human form to emerge onto the beach I felt like Ursula Andress in *Dr. No*. I didn't know at the time that I'd forgotten to shake myself out of a side fin.

Margaret is Most Welcoming

A woman called Margaret Rivers was there to welcome me. Margaret looked a lot like Joan Rivers, and I wondered if she might be a long-lost relation. She said she'd heard I was on my way while listening to whale sound.
Margaret showed me around the picturesque post-surfie community, and then made me dinner. She also let me use her computer, and I was delighted to see Green had read my previous blog and relayed it to readers of the *Greenygrey* website.
We also managed to contact my whale shark companions. They sent greetings on their return journey as I prepared for bed, and their relaxing melodies guaranteed me a good night's kip.

Notes

kip – slang for sleep.
Ursula Andress (actress).
Dr. No (Bond film).
Joan Rivers (comedienne).

4. BRUNCHING ON BUNS BURIED IN BUNBURY

I bade farewell to Margaret Rivers at first light, and Margaret River at third; refreshed after wonderful winks that far exceeded forty.

Roadrunner to Bunbury

It was a beautiful sunny morning and I felt like cruising down the highway with the wind in my hair. So I shapeshifted into a roadrunner and picked up some speed. However, this of course meant the wind was in my feathers, which wasn't quite the same; and I also felt like a bit of a turncoat against my ol' hero, Wile E. Coyote.
Nevertheless, it was a most enjoyable journey down the freeway, and I arrived in Bunbury in time for brunch. The name of the city made me bun hungry, and I looked for a bakery after changing into a human. I thought a roadrunner looking for food in the middle of a surprisingly large metropolis would have raised at least one eyebrow too many.

Buried Buns in the Bunbury Basement

I thought Bunbury would be full of bakeries, but a local called Rose Hotel told me they were called bunneries in Bunbury; and they were all underground on the edge of town to keep them cool in the hot summers.
So I hiked to the edge of town, and lo and behold, found big basement bunneries serving the most delicious cool fresh buns. The benefit of burying buns was confirmed on first bite.

Dipping into the Dolphin Discovery Centre

While bun-munching by the counter I got talking to a dolphin called Dolly; she had swum up from Koombanna Bay (the bunnery had land, sea and air entrances). Dolly said Koombanna is an idyllic spot, and invited me over.

So I shapeshifted into a dolphin after my last bite of bun, and spent a wonderful evening swimming in the cool Koombanna waters with a dozen dolphins.

Yes, it had been some day, fitting in roadrunning and dolphining either side of biting through a baker's dozen of Bunbury's best buried buns.

As I drifted on the ocean waves under a starry moonlit night in that twilight time between sleepiness and slumber I could hear the cetaceans clicking under the water and thought I heard dogs barking above it from the distant shore. The latter would soon lead me on another amazing adventure.

Notes

Cetacean – large marine mammal, such as whale, dolphin and porpoise.

There is a Rose Hotel in Bunbury.

Wile E. Coyote (cartoon coyote).

----

5. TRAVELLING THE AUSTRALIAN OUTBACK LIKE KEROUAC

After awakening into a bright sunny morning I again heard the haunting howling lullabies that seemed to be sailing across the waves and straight down my lugholes.
Dolly and the other dolphins were heading out to open sea, so I wished them luck and bade them farewell before heading towards land.

Smell or Sound, Buns or Hound

My senses were thrown into chaos when I reached the shore. From the north wafted an aroma that promised breakfast buns, while inland to the east there was a lyrical libretto lullaby that sounded like it could be a lapdog and Labrador rendition of *Les Miserables*.
This time, my canine curiosity won the decision of direction debate, and I made a scramble to ramble despite my belly grumbling and a rumbling.

Florida Reminder

I took my time as I headed across the South Western Highway. A snake slithering in the opposite direction reminded me of the floor rider in Florida that Green and I met on our North American ramble. There was no communication this time, and the barking of dogs from over the eastern horizon was the only sound that pierced the 360 degree silence.
An hour later, I reached a sign declaring *Welcome to the Collie Town Limits*. Was the dog sounding town the source of the canine sounds?

Notes

Jack Kerouac (writer).
Les Miserables (musical).

6. GREY'S ANATOMY PLOT EXPOSED BY COLLIE TWINS

The barking grew louder as I continued toward town, and then Collie came into view through the hazy heat. I thought I'd take the hint and shapeshift into a collie; choosing a border shape from a surprisingly large choice. When I'd completed the shift, Grey's anatomy had changed to black and white.

Famous Collies on the Edge of Town

As I reached Collie, a Shetland sheepdog rushed past carrying a lassie over its shoulders; it looked like a daring rescue was underway.
A babey pig then flew over my head squealing, 'Fly - Fly'; followed by another border collie running along underneath.

Meeting the Collie Twins: Colin and Ollie

When I reached the edge of Collie I was met by a couple of dogs guarding the town entrance.

They asked who I might be,
I replied a border collie,
as it should be plain to see.
And who may thee be,
I did respondee.

The bearded one said their names were Colin and Ollie McNab: respected and renowned around these parts as the Collie twins. They said their mother is an Australian stumpy tail cattle dog collie, and their recently departed father was part McNab shepherd collie and part bearded collie.
I said it was a pleasure to make their acquaintance.
They apologised for putting me under scrutiny, before explaining that Collie was a big bun-mining town; supplying Bunbury with most of its buns. The benefits of living on top of such a bountiful basement were unfortunately a double-

edged sword, as the bun bonanza also attracted desperados desperate to get their meddlesome mitts on the munchable minerals that can be moulded into muffins without needing a Midas touch.

Grey's Anatomy Plot Exposed

The Collie twins sniffed around my person with sensitive security. I was a little nervous, and this escalated into panic when Colin asked how long I had been a collie.
I didn't want to fib to such fine upstanding collies, so I explained my situation: how I had shapeshifted into a collie after hearing the barking and seeing the town was called Collie.
I waited with bated breath for the Collie response.

Notes

lassie – slang for female.
Grey's Anatomy (TV series).
*Babe (*film about a pig*)*.
*Lassie (*dog series and film*)*.
----

7. LASSIE COMES HOME TO SAVE THE DAY FOR THE FADE TO GREY

The Collie twins whispered amongst themselves, before telling me they thought my story sounded suspicious. They had heard of the legendary Greenygreys, but one hadn't been seen in these parts for many a century, and they had never heard of one dividing into Green and Grey. I was starting to think the game was up, but then the Shetland sheepdog I'd seen earlier returned.

Saved by a Hero

It introduced itself as Lassie, and said that with its fantastic hearing ability it had overheard part of our conversation. Lassie then got me off the hook by telling the Collies that it recognised me as one half of the Greenygrey from *I'm A Celebrity Werewolf...Get Me Out of Here*. It had been studying the programme on the Full Moon Satellite Channel for a part in an upcoming film, so had taken particular notice.

I then realised it was THE Lassie, legendary Hollywood star. I felt full-on flabbergastation to have met a fellow celebrity way out in the outback; to be saved by a dog that I'd admired for so long because of its saving ability was like a dream come true.

Colin and Ollie relaxed once Lassie had saved the day,
and welcomed me to Collie with tails awaggay,
I shapeshifted back, slowly fading to Grey,
we entered the town, with Lassie leading the way.

Collie is Proud of its Colliering

I saw at once how proud Collie is of its colliering. While many of their buns are exported to Bunbury, they also keep enough to feed all the Collie collies. Lassie took me to some of the finest bunneries Collie has to offer, and we feasted on bunches of buns. I think my favourite was the collar bone collie bun, which was the shape of a collar bone, and came in several different sizes; such as collie, wolf and human.

In the afternoon, we visited the Wellington National Park for a scenic forest and river walk. I was surprised it was so green, and that of course reminded me of my Green other half. I hoped ol' Green was still okay back home. We frequented the Bunfields Museum in the evening, where there were bun-mining exhibits going back centuries.

Lassie provided shelter that night, and as we chatted until late my plans changed. I'd said I was heading to Perth next, but Lassie suggested I detour to the small town of Latham, which it considered quite interesting.

The name reminded me of our ol' partner, Marc Latham, so I thought I'd take Lassie's advice. It's funny how travel plans can change overnight. Well, maybe not that funny; in humorous terms anyway. Sometimes I forget this is supposed to be a comedy!

Notes

The town of Collie has a coalfields museum.
I'm a Celebrity Get Me Out of Here (reality television show).

----

8. LATHAM IS WEIRD OFF THE RAILS

I left Lassie in limbo; between saving me and the next lucky one. I waved back at my hero-dog as I left Collie and headed out on the road to Latham. I walked for hours, but never really felt like I was getting nearer: like some things you just can't reach.

I also passed signs for a more direct route to Perth on the way, and wondered if I'd made the right decision; but Latham did sound somewhat interesting.

Walking All Over Latham

I decided to shapeshift into an emu, and the decision did not seem bird-brained, as I at last felt like I was getting somewhere. I reached Latham without knowing it in the end, because the welcome sign said MAHTAL rather than LATHAM, like in some kind of a mirror effect. My bird-brain surprised me when it worked it out before reaching the town centre. I shifted back into human shape soon after.

The town seemed nice when I got inside, with lots of people happily playing sports and doing fun things in forested parks and pristine lakes.

However, then I crossed the tracks and it didn't seem as rosy over the other side, with lots of people surviving in the sewers and slaving in sweat shops; this not surprisingly led to a rather depressing atmosphere. I felt more at home on this side of the tracks funnily enough. I think Green would have preferred the other.

Twentieth-Century British People Used as Forced Labour

A ball fell into my path, and I kicked it back to its owners. We got talking, and after I told them of my exiling experience they said they could relate to it, as they had been promised *Oranges and Sunshine* before being sent away as child migrants fifty years ago.

They said they had been used as forced labour, which was something I thankfully hadn't had to endure. Life had improved for them now, and they took me to their local pub for lunch. I found it difficult to leave; not having anywhere else to go.

I awoke on the edge of town.

Notes

In *Cool Hand Luke* there is a famous quote including the line *'Some men you just can't reach'*. It was later used by Guns N' Roses to introduce their *Civil War* song. *Oranges and Sunshine* tells the story of poor British 'Home Children' being sent from the UK to suffer abuse and forced labour in Commonwealth countries from the 1860s to 1970s. They were promised bright futures before leaving.

---

9. THE WISDOM OF ANTS IS PANTS WHEN HUNGOVER

It had all gone weird in Latham, and I seemed to have lost track of self, space and time.

Hearing Voices

I tried to rise, but felt groggy and my head hurt, so I lay back down. Then I heard something say: 'You think you're big, don't you.'
I looked up and could see nothing around. I thought I must be hearing voices in my confused state.
But then I heard it again: 'You think you're big, don't you.' And this time it was followed by: 'Oi, you big bundle of grey fluff, you think you're big don't you, you can't even see me down here.'

Antstronauts Anyone

I looked down and saw an ant. It was carrying a massive weight on its back, and working hard herding aphids. I felt quite guilty, sleeping off a hangover, while that wee chap was working so hard.
I didn't know what to say, and it soon went on its way. I returned to the land of nod, dreaming of antstronauts exploring the universe.

10. FOLLOWING EAGLES TO THE HOTEL CALIFORNIA

I awoke still on the edge of Latham. I was beginning to think I only existed in Latham.

Viewing Latham from the Other Side

Hunger and thirst finally inspired my return to the town centre. The sign was the right way round this time, clearly spelling out: LATHAM.
As I returned to where I'd been before, I saw the same people playing football. Their ball went flying off the pitch to the other side, landing at the feet of what looked like another me. The 'other me' kicked it back, before talking with the players. Then they all went to the same pub we'd frequented.

Eagles and the Hotel California

I felt perplexed, and thought I'd better find somewhere to chill out and get my mind right. I looked up into the hazy midday heat. A couple of eagles seemed to be leading me somewhere; waving their wings in a southerly direction. I followed them until they flew down and rested on a hotel called California. I thought it was a strange name for an establishment in Western Australia, but I suppose it isn't that extraordinary really. I rented a room and went straight to bed.

Notes

Getting the mind right is another *Cool Hand Luke* theme. The strange events in Latham were probably inspired by shows like *The Prisoner, Twin Peaks, Lost* and *American Gothic.*
Eagles and song (*Hotel California*). There's no Hotel California in the town of Latham as far as the author knows.

11. IS BRITAIN SUNNY NOW? GREY DREAMS AND NIGHTMARES

I seemed to sleep for an age. I dreamt the Greenygrey world was sunny all the time now I wasn't there, and everything lived joyously under neverending blue skies. I envisaged Blighty being so brighty that stars dropped to Earth in the form of birds to re-energise their glows amongst the overabundance of sparkling effervescence.

I also wondered if my other half Green had forgotten me already, and joined with blue and yellow, which are after all its constituent colours.

And what about my lookalike. Was it connected to me, or was it another me? Was there a message I should understand? Bird-brain or going insane, it all seemed such a pain.

I awoke feeling sick and soaked in sweat. It was all still a mystery.

12. ANIMALS VISIT WEREWOLF GREY TO SAVE THE DAY

Lassie, Lassie, is that you Lassie? I was in turmoil, and Lassie was bouncing around my mind like it leapt along mountain passes when at its Hollywood peak. *Lassie, Lassie, where are you leading me? Lassie, Lassie, what are you trying to tell me? Lassie, Lassie, can I trust you, or are you a false guide?*

Animals tell me to Leave Latham

My mind saw Lassie in a musical band with other animals I'd met on my journey. The Hollywood dog was on vocals; Vombat the wombat on guitar; Digger the dingo on bass, and Dolly the dolphin on drums.
When I heard them singing *We Just Gotta Get Out Of This Place* I thought there was a message in there somewhere, but I couldn't quite grasp it... until I got it... Lassie was trying to lead me out of Latham.

Lassie's Message not Nonsense

Lassie's message inspired me to crawl out of bed and attempt to leave. I was shocked to see the foyer was full of my lookalikes. I asked one how long it had been here. It said it arrived one day after me. Was it the one I saw having the same experience as me? I couldn't tell. I asked another. It said it arrived two days after me. Yes, the next one said three days after me.
I guessed the next one would say four days, but didn't want to investigate further; I just wanted to leave. I stumbled toward the door. It opened first time to my relief and surprise. I emerged into sunshine having escaped Latham's *Hotel California*.
The same Eagles that had led me to the hotel were flying above. Didn't the Eagles band sing about not being able to leave a *Hotel California*? It was quite a coincidence if they did.

I found the road leading in a northerly direction and started walking. The Eagles seemed to follow me. It looked a long road out of Latham, but after a few hours I could see the town no more.

Notes

Animals and song *(We Just Gotta Get Out of this Place)*. Eagles and song *(Long Road out of Eden)*.

---

13. PRINCE MEETS PINK FLOYD THROUGH PIGEON COOING

The desert chose my direction, or at least limited my options; I was heading to north and new, and the alternative was south and scary. I was happy to be. Just to be. To be without decisions, pressures and stress. To be the only life I could see. To be able to sing thinking I was in harmony; without anyone to contradict me. Although my feet kept to the road, my mind flew this way and that; to the north, west, south and east horizons; looking north to the future, south at the past, and wondering about what I have missed and will miss to the east and west. Sometimes my thoughts settled into the outback, nothing in nothingness; it was a nice place to be.

Pigeons Line the Coorow Road

As I approached Coorow on the Coorow Road, there were hundreds of pigeons on either side of my route. They were cooing a poem that rang a bell somewhere in my mind, so my brain was hearing a repetitive: 'ding, dong, coo, coo, ding, dong, coo, coo.'
I wasn't too amused at first, and thought the town could do with a coup to stop all the cooing, but then it began to sound sweeter and more melodic the more I heard it.
I finally worked out that it was Marc Latham's *Pigeons on the Wing* they were reciting; a poem written from a pigeon point of view ending on a high with the lines:

'Through blue skies to green trees,
where we coo in peace.'

Notes

As well as the author's own travel experiences, Jack Kerouac and Paul Theroux's travel memoirs probably inspired the first paragraph, although the author had not read either's

writing for eight months beforehand.
Prince and song (*When Doves Cry*).
Pink Floyd and song (*Pigs on the Wing*).

----

14. GREY TAKES GREY ROAD TO GREY

I gathered momentum after passing Coorow, and was soon on the Green Head Road. This of course reminded me of my other half Green, and I became quite nostalgic once again. At least it took my mind off Latham, which was pushed to the extremities of my memories.

Greyt Welcome for Grey in Grey

I was making good progress toward Perth when I found myself on the Grey Road to Grey. Unbelievable I know, but true and totally unplanned! If I was writing pure fiction I wouldn't dare include it! It's finding hidden little treasures like this that keep the magic of virtual travelling alive for me. When I entered Grey there was another surprise (purely fictional this time!), because there were welcome signs for me everywhere. One read: 'The Grey is Greyt'; while another went a little too far for my liking, although it did sound rather tasty: 'The Grey is Veggie Gravy Filled with Fried Onions on Top of Mashed Potato and Mushrooms.' I appreciated the thought all the same... and the recipe.
We had a greyt night.

15. DON QUIXOTE AND SANCHO PANZA FROM CERVANTES

I left Grey feeling glad to be Grey. I thought I could whizz down to Perth in no time, but fancied more company, so I hitch-hiked from Cervantes.

Don Quixote and Sancho Panza from Cervantes

I had only stuck my thumb out for a minute or two when an old camper-van pulled up, and a guy shouted: 'Hola greyngo, you wanna de lift, come on pronto.'
I needed no more invitation, and rushed to the van before hopping in. The driver introduced himself as Sancho Panza, and his more cavalier passenger as Don Quixote.
They said they had been in Cervantes all their lives, so it felt good to be out and about.

Jo Brand and Russell Brand on the Brand Highway

As we drove down the Brand Highway we saw an odd-looking couple hitching south. Sancho picked them up as well. The hitchers introduced themselves as Jo and Russell Brand. It didn't take long before they were cracking jokes left, right and centre, so it turned out to be a fun ride.
Although it meant more room for me, I was quite sad when we dropped the Brands off on the edge of the Badginarra National Park. They said they were going to stay with a band of badgers.
The van calmed down a little after that, but was still very jolly, with Don jumping about to Midnight Oil and Men at Work music.

The Edge of Perth

We whizzed along the edge of Perth, passing Cataby, which was full of cats; Orange Springs, which was very orange; and the Moore River National Park, which had less river than I expected.

I don't know what was going on in Beermullah; it seemed confused. That was not the case with Banksia Grove, where artistic paintings told a clear story.

We arrived in Perth with space and time having sped by, and many great memories stored in my noggin.

Notes

Hitching can be dangerous.

noggin – slang for head.

Sancho Panza and Don Quixote (fictional characters created by Cervantes, which is also the name of a Western Australia town).

Jo Brand and Russell Brand (British comedienne and comedian).

Midnight Oil and Men at Work (Aussie bands).

Banksy (British artist).

----

16. ROCKING IT AT THE ROCK-IT FESTIVAL IN PERTH

Sancho and Don said they were off to the Rock-It festival in Perth, and invited me along. I jumped at the chance; metaphorically of course, because I was in the car at the time.

I felt like I needed a bit of fun after a tough time in Latham, and they seemed to be in the same situation having just escaped Cervantes.

Rock-It Festival in Perth

We had difficulty finding the Joondalup area where Rock-It is held, and had to do a loop around the neck of the Swan River. However, once we entered the festival it really rocked. Tracer started the day off for us with some fantastic space rock. They were followed by a storming Airbourne set, and a great slide-guitar fuelled bluesy show by Rose Tattoo. Brian Johnson era AC/DC played a solid set, and nicely warmed us up for a sensational Bon Scott era AC/DC bad boy boogie headlining show.

Relaxing on Rotto: Rottnest Island

We were hot and sweaty after the show, so we headed out to Rottnest Island; or Rotto as it's known locally. There was certainly nothing rotten about it, and we enjoyed the beautiful beaches on the unspoilt island.

We were joined by some quirky quokkas: animals that are to kangaroos what greenygreys are to werewolves. They were lots of fun, and provided great company before we fell asleep under the rising sun.

Notes

Quokka - a small macropod (marsupial family Macropodidae) about the size of a domestic cat.

Rock-It Festival in Perth.
Tracer, Airbourne, Rose Tattoo, AC/DC (Aussie bands).
Bon Scott and Brian Johnson (AC/DC vocalists).
----

17. BONZO SCOTTIE ON THE HIGHWAY TO LANCELIN

I said adios to Don and Sancho in the morning, before heading up the highway. Not long after, I saw a ghostly dog apparition hitch-hiking.

Bonzo Scottie Joins the Ozyssey

I greeted it when I reached it. It introduced himself as Bonzo Scottie, before asking if this was the *Highway to Hell*. I replied that I was a stranger in these parts, but didn't think so; as far as I knew, it was the highway to Lancelin, which didn't sound much like Hell. Poor Bonzo seemed upset, as if he had the *Downpayment Blues*. He said he thought he'd been *stripped of his soul*, and that he might find it in *Hell, which ain't supposed to be a bad place to be.*
I said I thought searching for Hell should be the last resort, and I didn't think it was up ahead, but he was quite welcome to *Ride On* with me.

Yoko Ono of Lancelin

Bonzo agreed, and cheered up on the way to Lancelin; we seemed to reach it in no time. Upon arrival, we met a sea lion called Celia Ono, and she recommended the windsurfing, dune buggying and sandboarding that were very popular on the pristine beaches.
We didn't need much arm-twisting, and had a fabulous afternoon and evening enjoying the beach sports. Celia had great balance, and I had to laugh when Bonzo exclaimed that the *Girl's got Rhythm.*

Notes

AC/DC songs: *Highway to Hell, Downpayment Blues, Soul Stripper, Hell Ain't A Bad Place To Be, Ride On, Girl's got*

Rhythm.
Yoko Ono (artist and musician).

----

18. CALLING KALBARRI BARRY LEADS TO DOLPHINIAN DETOUR

We said goodbye to Celia in the morning and got back on the road. It wasn't long before we passed my town namesake, Grey. Travelling the Grey Road out of Grey was a joy, and I once more felt glad to be Grey.

Kalbarri Calamity Averted

We kept ahead of schedule all day, so I thought I'd call Barry the Bottlenose Dolphin when we reached Kalbarri; Dolly had given me his number, and said he was often in west coast waters. I don't know what inspired me to call Barry in Kalbarri.

I shapeshifted into a dolphin again and sent out some long-range clicks, but Barry replied that he was out with the family on an ocean safari off Jungulu Island.

However, it wasn't a totally wasted call, because he warned me there was a storm heading our way, and recommended heading inland. He said there was a friendly meerkat community in Meekatharra that would help us on our way. The horizon was looking grey. Although I half wanted to meet the storm, and see if I fitted in with it, I didn't feel it was fair to Bonzo; and the meerkat community did sound fascinating. So we took Barry's advice and headed inland.

19. ORLOVS OF OZ SUFFER MONOTHEISTIC MADNESS

The storm seemed to be catching up with us, so I shapeshifted into a flying elephant, which is one of the hardest single-species shapeshifts to accomplish. Looking back on it, I was probably showing off in front of Bonzo; or below him to be more exact. My new friend hung on to my ears for dear life as we flew high over the Kalbarri National Park, which looked so beautiful I somewhat regretted not being on the ground.

A couple of hours later I caught sight of Meekatharra for the first time, but couldn't see any meerkats; I was sure Barry said there was a big community. All I could see was a single human, who seemed to be ranting.

I started to descend slowly, but the storm caught up with us just afterwards. I was spun out of control and we were soon falling like a rock and pebble; until I landed trunk-up on the human. Bonzo was sent sprawling, but was back on his feet before me. I shapeshifted out of elephant first.

The Meerkats Emerge from Hiding

I felt awful to have landed on the human, and Bonzo was distraught. I felt better when masses of meerkats emerged from hiding and seemed to start celebrating with a song that went something like: 'ding-dong, the monotheist has been put to bed, the monotonous monotheist has been put to bed...'

I was still shocked though, and asked the meerkats what they were so happy about. A couple introduced themselves as Bruce and Sheila Orlov, before telling me their story.

The Meerkat-Monotheistic History

They said most of their family had settled in Meerkovo after emigrating from Africa, but they had continued to Oz; building an idyllic meerkat community amongst the wonderful nature in this area. Then a monotonous monotheist (MoMo) arrived, introducing itself as enaB. The MoMo persuaded them to cut all the trees down to build a big new temple, promising them that it would safeguard their future.

There were no problems during the next decade, and they thought they'd done the right thing, but then the rains came. With all the trees chopped down there was nothing to stop flooding in the area. This also polluted the river, so they were left without food and water, and needed to call on their reserves to save the community.

That was when they found out the MoMo had traded all their riches, and left the area while they tried to survive the disaster. It had used its money to grow ever more powerful, and they had been hiding from it ever since. So they felt liberated from a great evil.

I said I knew how they felt after my recent experiences in the Greenygrey world.

Notes

Grey's elephant flight with Bonzo is reminiscent of Disney's Dumbo and Timothy Q. Mouse.
Wizard of Oz, Wicked Witch of the West (classic film and character).
Orlovs (Compare the Market [Meerkat] advert characters live in Meerkovo).

----

20. MEERKATS-MONOTHEISTS MIX MAKES MAD MORNING

I had just about absorbed all that information, when another human dropped from the sky in a *Porcelain* pod. I hoped it wasn't more trouble; I'd had enough for one day!
The human burst out singing: '*Hallelujah*, I am Mildly Monotheistic Moby (MiMo Moby), and I'm *Feeling So Real*. I know *Everything Was Wrong Here*, but now that the *Sky Has Broken* and the Grey descended, the Monotonous Monotheists must *Go*, and matters return to magic for the meerkats of Meekatharra.'
When I heard him say Monotonous Monotheists in the plural my heart sank; either he'd messed up his lines or there was more than one.

Wizard of Oz First Witch Meeting Scene

It wasn't long before my fears were realised. I heard a monotonous murmuring sound coming from somewhere, and it grew louder with every second. The meerkats dived for cover, and Bonzo covered his ears. When the orator came into view I saw it looked like the human I'd landed on. It approached us.
'Ah, Monotonous Monotheist of the East (MoMo East), I thought you might arrive soon,' said MiMo Moby.
So there was another one; my heart sank deeper than before. The meerkats were nowhere to be seen, and Bonzo belted out the blues.
'Aah, hah,' MoMo East ranted, 'you might have stopped my Western twin from controlling your lives, but I am the stronger of the two, and I will wreak rampant revenge upon your sinning souls, just you wait and see, aah, hah!'
As it stopped cackling it sprang towards its twin's head, but MiMo Moby somehow transported an emerald cork hat from the MoMo West's head onto my bonce before the MoMo East could reach it.
MoMo East turned with a look of hellfire on its face.

MiMo Moby took no pity, shouting, '*Go*, you have no power in Meekatharra.'

MoMo East cackled out another rant and repeated the threat before vanishing as quickly as it had appeared.

Before also leaving, MiMo congratulated the meerkats on their liberation, and told Bonzo and me, 'You have done a good deed here today, and should now follow the dust sandy path. The path will be difficult, and full of tests, but will ultimately lead you to the Great Dame of Oz. She should help you complete your epic rambling quest. Take great care of the hat, as it is very precious and has magical powers that will be useful on the dust sandy path. It must not fall into the wrong hands. Let it rest peacefully on your bonce, for there is more than you can imagine resting on it.'

Notes

Cork hats are traditional Aussie bush headgear.
bonce - slang for head.
Moby and songs: *Porcelain, Hallelujah, Feeling So Real, Everything Is Wrong, Sky Has Broken, Go.*
Wicked Witch of the East (character in *Wizard of Oz*).

----

21. NEWMAN'S COOL HAND LUKE ARRESTED PERFORMANCE

With the Momo East departed, a sudden wave of fresh nature seemed to spring into Meekatharra, and all the meerkats started dancing in the streets. Bruce said they were dancing flamboyantly because it had been banned under monotheist rule, so they hadn't done it in public for a long time.

It was fantastic to see them enjoying themselves, and I hoped they would live their lives in freedom and peace from henceforth.

Ned Kelly and Paul Newman

When the dancing had calmed, and the meerkats were preparing to eat, we bade them farewell and left to continue our journey.

Thankfully, there was only one more significant event that day. Passing through Newman, we witnessed a *Butch Hustler* being arrested for damaging a fire hydrant. The officer said, '*Luke Cassidy*, my name is Sheriff Ned Kelly, and I am arresting you for laying a *cool hand* on county property.'

Luke looked down on his luck, but was still smiling. Bonzo smiled back.

Notes

Paul Newman and films he starred in: *Butch Cassidy and the Sundance Kid, The Hustler, Cool Hand Luke*. In the latter, his character, Luke, is arrested at the start for damaging a fire hydrant; and despite all his problems (being shot, possibly fatally) he is still smiling at the end.

Ned Kelly (19th century Aussie bushranger).

----

22. KARIJINI CURRY GENIE SERVES UP VIDEO CONFERENCE

We reached Karijini by mid-morning. Fancying a spicy brekkie, we popped into a curry house. A fellow from a neighbouring town called Tom Price provided great service.

The Karijini Curry Genie

We were half-way through a veggie vindaloo when a genie emerged from between the pilau and potato. It rose above us before declaring that it could grant one wish a day; one of us could have the wish today.

Bonzo said I could have the wish, as he was a bit of a lost soul, and didn't know what he wanted. I thanked Bonz, before telling the genie I'd like to talk to my other half if possible; the one (half) and only Green.

Genie Grants my Green Wish

The curry genie was as good as its word, and by the time we'd finished off the colourful kulfi I was talking to my other half by video conference. It was great to talk to Green, and it didn't seem off colour at all.

We relaxed the rest of the day, and slept overnight in a Karijini caravan.

Notes

Tom Price is the name of a town near Karijini.
Genie (character in *Aladdin*).

----

23. KIMBERLEY HOSTS ROBIN HOOD SCENERY

We made consistent progress on the dust sandy path in the morning, and arrived in Broome by lunchtime.

Bathing with Beagles and Buying Brooms in Broome

We were dusty and sandy, so we agreed a dip in Beagle Bay seemed a good idea. It was a beautiful day, and the beach was full of beagles by the time we got there. I talked to one called Biggles, and he said they were mostly recuperating after taking part in smoking tests. The sea air and swimming were supposed to be good for their breathing.

After bidding the beagles bye-bye we set off on the path once again. On the edge of Broome we met a broom salesman by the side of the road. Bonzo said we should buy a broom, as they were pretty cheap, and it might come in handy on the dust sandy path. So we purchased one, and it sure did come in handy.

Fitzroy Makes Bonzo go TNT

We reached Fitzroy Crossing by evening, but a man waving a staff around stopped us crossing a log bridge into town. He bellowed, 'Nobody can cross this bridge past Fitzroy.'

Bonzo had obviously had enough for one day, and screamed at Fitzroy with the ferocity of an AC/DC back catalogue, 'I don't have time for *Beating Around the Bush* with a *Cold Hearted Man; If You Want Blood You've Got It.*' Then he seemed to charge the broom up to *High Voltage* before launching it at Fitzroy.

The broom flew through the air and hit Fitzroy's eye with a bullseye, knocking him off the log and into the river below. Bonzo turned to me and said it had been a *Shoot to Thrill*, and that *Dirty Deeds Done Dirt Cheap* were sometimes necessary.

We crossed the river, and passed through Fitzroy Crossing. A fair maiden welcomed us on the other side. She said her name was Kimberley, and this land was named after her.

Notes

Kimberley is a region in the north of Western Australia.
Scenes in the movie *Australia* were filmed there.
Robin Hood and other characters in the story: Little John
and Maid Marian.
AC/DC songs: *Beating Around the Bush, Cold Hearted Man,
If You Want Blood You've Got It, High Voltage, Shoot to
Thrill, Dirty Deeds Done Dirt Cheap, TNT.*

---

24. BOGOL IN THE NORTHERN TERRITORY

Kimberley showed us the way through her land, and took us to the edge of the Northern Territory. We thanked her and bade her farewell, before going farther into the outback.

Kermy's Kermits Copy Herman's Hermits

We grabbed a few hours sleep in the late morning, before running with the road trains in the early afternoon. We reached Nitmiluk at tea-time. There were rollicking rhapsodies emitting from a tavern in the middle of town called *The One More Before I Croak*, so we thought we'd enter for a drink or three.
It turned out to be a wise decision, because a frog fivesome Herman's Hermits copy band called Kermy's Kermits were belting out classic croak n' roll tunes on stage.

Knit Me Luck in Nitmiluk

It started to get chilly in the evening, so we went shopping for extra clothing. It didn't take long to find a cheap sheep shop. Moreover, it had a buy one knitted jumper and get one knitted for luck offer. It sounded like an interesting variation on the BOGOF (Buy One Get One Free) theme: more BOGOL. It seemed ideal for me and Bonzo to get one each. So we did indeed partake in the offer, and Bonzo had a jumper knitted for luck by a serenely sleepy sheep called Siddharta.

Notes

Kermit the Frog (Muppets character).
Herman's Hermits (1960s band).
Siddharta (the original Buddha).
----

25. HUMPTY DOO AND THE QUACK I DO IN KAKADU

We departed Nitmiluk in the morning, warmly encased in our BOGOL jumpers. Bonzo said he felt limitlessly lucky, and there seemed no limits to our progress on the path, as we reached the Kakadu National Park in no time.

Nice Surprise at Alligator Wildman

Bonzo and I freshened up at the waterfall where the Wildman and Alligator rivers met, as we didn't fancy meeting the Wildman or Alligator on their own; our consensus theory was that they'd be too pre-occupied with each other at the waterfall to take any notice of us.
We were just emerging from the water when an extraordinary looking creature arrived on the beach. Its head reminded me of my ol' hero Scooby Doo, but it seemed to have an egg body like that of Humpty Dumpty.
It was accompanied by a duck that always seemed to be whistling.

Ready for the Quack I Do in Kakadu?

The duck approached us and whistled, 'Hello, I am Dr. Darwin, a local whistler duck quack, and this is my friend, the Humpty Doo, who also lives nearby. We have ventured east to Kakadu hoping to discover new species. We thought you might be of some interest, but we have concluded that you are both old species. Although there hasn't been a werewolf seen in these parts for many a century.'
I returned the greeting, and thanked them for their interest, before saying I'd never seen a Humpty Doo before. Dr. Darwin said Humpty was an interesting creature, and he wasn't sure how he'd evolved; it was ongoing research, but his theory on the origin of species was that the Humpty Doo was descended from an English civil war rhyme and a Hollywood cartoon dog.

So maybe I was right. I was excited, and asked if it really believed this. For the first time it did not whistle its opinion; instead it did quack, 'I do.'

Notes

Darwin and Humpty Doo are Northern Territories towns.
Scooby Doo (cartoon dog).
Humpty Dumpty (English civil war nursery rhyme character).
Charles Darwin (19th century scientist, and his book: *On The Origin of Species*).

---

26. MORE ADVENTURES FOR BOGOL

I enquired if they knew of a nice southerly
journey. Darwin whistled thoroughly
recommending visiting Jabiru
in the centre of Kakadu
so we travelled there
with the pair.
Do try the bread, said Humpty Doo,
so I had a sarnie, and Bonzo had two.

No Handbags Alligator Fight

After eating and saying our goodbyes, Darwin and Humpty
left to look for new species, while we continued south.
It didn't take us long to reach Nitmiluk again. We checked
out our favourite boozer, *The One More Before I Croak*,
which had a hop going on. There was a poster above the bar
advertising an alligator eliminator fight at the No Handbags
bar, so after a drink we checked it out. And water fight it was,
with Freshwater Frank beating Saltwater Stan in what could
not be described as a toothless tussle.

Kathy and Baloo Wonder if Nitmiluk is too Good to be True

With a little time to spare, we returned to the cheap sheep
shop. A koala called Kathy from Katherine and a man called
Baloo from Manbulloo were getting BOGOL jumpers knitted.

They thought the deal was too good to be true,
but were reassured after we showed them our two,
and informed them of our luck in meeting Humpty Doo
and whistler duck Darwin in Kakadu.

When we told them we were following the dust sandy path
south, Kathy dropped her new jumper. Baloo picked it up for
her, before warning us we might need more luck if we were

heading that way, as they'd heard it had become quite hellish in the outback.

Notes

sarnie – slang for sandwich.

----

27. FINDING ELLE ON THE HIGHWAY TO HELL

Bonzo didn't like the sound of that, not fancying hell anymore, and rushed off to buy another two jumpers. Once he was wearing them, he said, 'They might bring more luck on the *Highway to Hell*, and anyway, it *Ain't No Fun Waiting Round To Be A Millionaire* in a *Dog Eat Dog* world.' He pulled his third jumper right up to his jaw, and I heard him whisper to it, 'I'm *Up To My Neck In You.*'
We said our Nitmiluk goodbyes, and Bonzo pulled his jumper down far enough to show a big smile. I smiled back, before we headed out into the unknowns of the outback.

Meeting Elle in Outback Hell

We left civilisation behind and headed into the outback. There was nothing but big wide open space ahead, and it all looked red; even the dust sandy path had an ochre coating. We travelled as fast as possible; like bats into hell.
I was beginning to question whether this could really be the correct direction for me to meet my destiny. It looked as if we were on the road to nowhere, and there was nothing of interest ahead.
That was until I saw a crouching human shape emerge out of the dust ahead. We stopped when we arrived in its proximity, and asked if we could be of assistance. It replied in a withering female voice that we should leave her, as she wasn't worth bothering about.

'Ell of a Job Persuading Elle

Bonzo and I looked at each other, before discussing the matter. We quickly decided that we couldn't leave her all alone in this harsh environment, and invited her along.
She refused at first, but Bonzo said we weren't going to leave without her. After a few minutes thinking, she said she would, but only for our sakes; because she couldn't slow us down any more than not starting.
We laughed, and welcomed her to our Ozyssey.

Notes

Bat Out of Hell (Meatloaf song).
Road to Nowhere (Talking Heads song).
Elle McPherson (model).
AC/DC songs: *Ain't No Fun Waiting Round To Be A Millionaire, Dog Eat Dog, Up To My Neck In You.*

----

28. BUNYIP SHENANIGANS AND SHINING EMERALDS

We continued south into the baking heat. There was no life visible anywhere, and only the dust sandy path kept us going... for mile after mile.

Then I saw something move in the distance. As we neared it, I realised it was a bunyip. I wondered what a bunyip was doing out in the desert, as they usually prefer swamps.

The Bunyip Asks Us to Play Ball

We stopped near the bunyip. Its breath wafted across the path, smelling like brontosaurus. At least it wasn't brachiosaurus; that is the worst.

I asked what a bunyip was doing in the arid Oz outback, so far from soggy swamps. It looked at us with mischievous eyes, and ignored my question. Instead, it invited us to play a game. We were in no rush, and had become intrigued, so agreed.

The bunyip then proceeded to theatrically roll three different coloured balls onto a fold-out table: one was green, another red and the last was pink. It said there was a prize to go with each ball, and we could choose one each: the prizes were green dye; a house and a new body.

Discussion and Deliberation Leads to Decision

The three of us entered into a huddle, trying our best not to muddle. I said it seemed an inviting offer, and I'd really like some green dye to make myself look greenygrey again. Bonzo agreed, and said he'd like a house; somewhere comfortable for when he settles down. Elle was also in favour; she said she'd like a new body, as she'd lost all confidence in herself. So we decided to play the game, thinking the green ball would be for the green dye prize; the red ball the house prize, and the pink ball the body prize.

Bunyip Shenanigans

We told the bunyip our choices, confident in our logic. The bunyip looked pleased with itself, laughing a big brontosaurus breath across the path. We knew why it felt smug when it announced that the green ball was for the family home; red was for the new body, and pink was for green dye.

I didn't need a new home as I wanted to return to the Greenygrey world; Bonzo didn't want a new body as it was happy being a Scottie, and Elle didn't think being dyed green would improve her body image.

So we started to swap prizes amongst each other, but the bunyip quickly intervened. It said there was a forfeit for exchanging the prizes, and the cost for three swaps was a hat. We only had the emerald cork hat. MiMo Moby said it had magical powers, but we hadn't seen any yet. So I took the hat off and said, 'Shine on you crazy emerald, or forever hold your peace.'

The hat started to glow, and then shone so much it was difficult to see anything amongst all the greenshine. But after a few seconds I could vaguely make out a figure appearing above. As the hat glow reduced in intensity I saw it was MiMo arriving. MiMo quickly warned us that the bunyip was really the surviving MoMo, trying to tempt us into giving it the emerald cork hat with prizes it thought we couldn't resist. Once it saw its ruse had been rumbled, the bunyip quickly changed into the MoMo we'd seen at Meekatharra. It ranted at us once more before flying off.

Notes

Bunyip - a large creature in Aboriginal mythology.
Shine On You Crazy Diamond (Pink Floyd song).
Kyle declared shenanigans in *South Park*'s *Cow Days* episode (season 2/episode 13, 1998).

----

29. ALICE SPRINGS IN THE DESERT

Before shooting off into the stratosphere, MiMo said 'Bonzo and Were, beware. Hold onto your hat and keep to the dust sandy path, unless the hat glows, because when it's safe it knows.'

We continued south. It seemed hellish to the east and west, and each side seemed to be pulling us its way. I tried to shut it out and continue progressing on the path.

Poor Bonzo was singing *Gimme a Bullet to Bite On*, while Elle said she was worried her body wasn't going to be strong enough to make it. I was struggling myself, and tried to think of a reunion with Green in the Greenygrey world to take my mind off the ordeal.

We were finding the going particularly tough late in the day, when suddenly a woman sprang out of the red sunset and landed on the path in front of us.

She introduced herself as Alice.

Notes

Gimme a Bullet to Bite On is an AC/DC song.

----

30. ALICE SPRINGS, WE SINGS AND THE WALLAROO SYMBS

'Come along off the path,' advised Alice, 'you all look plum pole-axed piqued out. The ghangiant could be along soon, and you don't want to be around when it turns up.'
I didn't like the sound of the ghangiant, and thought we'd had enough drama for one day. I checked the hat, and it was glowing, so we followed Alice:

Spring, spring, spring we span,
springing sprightly we sprang.

Alice Springs Invites us to Sing

We reached a spring, and Alice took a drink. She invited us to quench our thirst too, 'Come drink at this spring, it'll make you sing.' I checked the hat, and it was glowing, so I told the others it should be okay.
The water sure did taste sweet, and the next thing we knew, Bonzo was singing *Have a Drink on Me*. Elle then started singing *Waltzing Matilda,* before Warren Zevon's *Werewolves of London* must have cornered my cerebral cortex (nailed my noggin), because a rousing rendition suddenly burst out of my mouth. Alice finished off our medley with The Jam's *A Town Called Malice*.
'Why, Alice, I haven't heard such sweet singing since Sade stopped by the Springs,' a voice said from behind us. I looked around to see a macropod approaching.
'Hello Wally Mac,' exclaimed Alice, 'what brings a wallaroo like roo to these parts.'

Notes

cerebral cortex - outer layer of the brain; vital for thought processing.
noggin – slang for head.
Ghan - a passenger train operating on the Adelaide-Darwin

railway.

wallaroo - any of three closely related species between kangaroos and wallabies.

Have a Drink on Me (AC/DC song).

Waltzing Matilda (Australian bush ballad).

Werewolves of London (Warren Zevon song).

A Town Called Malice (The Jam song).

Sade (soul singer).

----

31. THE GREAT GIG IN THE SKY ABOVE ULURU / AYER'S ROCK

'I just came round to see if anybody fancied coming to the Oo-loo-roo Air's Rock festival at Uluru / Ayer's Rock this weekend. There are many magnificent macropod bands there. The way you're singing it sounds like you could even play there yourselves,' Wally answered.
'Thanks Wally,' Alice said laughing, 'Yeh, cobber, sounds fair dinkum me ol' bushie.'

The Great Gig in the Sky

After we'd had our fill of spring water we set off for the Oo-loo-roo Air's Rock festival. We were still springing, and now also singing, while Wally skipped. Apparently, all the macropods used to hop, until Skippy got them skipping in the 1960s.
After about an hour I saw a sensational sight in front of me, and thought it must be the Air's Rock venue, as there were several stages high up in the air. Each looked like a supersize space roocket the size of a desert view.
There was a portal entrance, and travelling up in it was quite an experience. After that, the good times just kept rolling, with an endless supply of amazing views and tunes. Bonzo looked like a butcher's dog for the first time.
I enjoyed quite a few bands, and especially the Roomones, Atomic Rooster and Roosh.
Atomic Rooster had a song called *Head in the Sky* which really suited the setting, while Roosh waited until darkness to play *Fly By Night*.
The Roomones played such a high energy set they seemed hopping mad. All the members are called Joey: the singer's moniker is Tribiani Joey; the guitarist is Smokin' Joey; the bassist is Guest Joey, and the drummer is Pesci Joey.
My favourite band was the headliners: Injured Wildlife. They had really socially conscious lyrics in songs like *Cousin Koala Curled Up In Eucalyptus* and *When Did You Last See a Waltzing Wallaby*. The entire crowd had a roousing sing-

along to the latter, and it was a fitting end to the great gig in the sky rookets.

Notes

Socially conscious band inspired by Midnight Oil, and especially their song, *Bed is Burning*. 'Injured Wildlife' name was inspired by an Aussie outback road sign image provided by Zemanta, which provides images for Wordpress blogs. cobber – Aussie slang for friend. fair dinkum - Aussie slang for true/real. bushie – Aussie slang for someone who lives in the bush.
Skippy (TV series kangaroo).
Ramones (punk/rock band. The original members all had pseudonyms with Ramone as their surname).
Atomic Rooster and song (*Head in the Sky*).
Rush and song (*Fly By Night*).
The Joeys: Joey Tribiani (*Friends* character), Smokin' Joe Frazier (boxer), Jo Guest (model), Joe Pesci (actor).

---

32. ELLE USES BODY

After returning to terra-firma we spent a couple more days with Alice and Wally before it felt time to move on. We thanked them for their hospitality, bade them farewell, and returned to the path.
There were none of the shenanigans we'd suffered before meeting Alice. Feeling chuffed with our progress, and thirsty too, we thought we'd stop for refreshments in the town of Hugh, although it wasn't huge.

Who's Who in Hugh's Who Bar?

We saw a bar called 'Who', which looked like the local celebrity hang-out, so we thought we'd give it a try.
Heath Ledger and Crocodile Dundee were drinking together at the bar. I asked them who else frequented Hugh's Who. Croc said Hugh Jackman used to pop in, but he now preferred Hugh's 'Here' bar.

Elle Carries Us to the Bush Telly

We got caught up in the friendly atmosphere at the bar, and it turned into a heavy day on the ol' amber nectar. Later on, everybody moved over to Hugh's 'There' bar for a nightcap. Hugh Jackman was there. I was surprised to see Hugh there in Hugh's 'There', as Croc had said he preferred Hugh's 'Here'.
Bonzo was worse for wear by the end of it, and I wasn't much better. Elle ended up carrying us both over to a bush telly they had burning on the edge of town.
I can't remember much there, but I remember asking 'Who's there?' when somebody bumped into me soon after I lay down... and the bush telly's flames making it look like there was a heavenly hue over Hugh's 'Here' bar.

Notes

bush telly – Aussie slang for a campfire.
Heath Ledger and Hugh Jackman (both actors).
Crocodile Dundee (fictional film and main character).

----

33. KNOWING ME, KNOWING YOU, ABBA IS THE BEST I CAN DO

We woke up feeling hungover in the morning; well, Bonzo and I did. I felt a little better after we cooked up a veggie brekkie on the rekindled bush telly.

Knowing Me, Knowing Hugh,

We called in the 'Who'
before leaving Hugh.
Croc and Heath were in there,
having a morning beer.
We joined them for a drink
and asked what do you think
about us leaving for the south?
Croc put hand to mouth.
He spent an eternity thinking,
so we just kept drinking,
with the suspense building.

The Poetry Must Stop

Croc must have sensed that, because the first thing he said was that there's a time for rhyme and another for straight talking. We knew he was serious when he started crying. Then he told us through crocodile tears that we'd have to get past the ghangiant to cross the border into South Australia. We had of course been warned about the ghangiant before, so I listened carefully to Croc's next words. He said we'd be alright if we travelled through the *Rainbow Valley* and found *Black Footed Rock Wally B*, as he had the key to our destiny for entering Oz South.
Heath said he'd tried to make the journey himself once, but the horizon never seemed to get closer until it overtook him.

Notes

Black-footed rock wallaby is a macropod species.
Blackfoot (rock band).

----

34. GREY'S DREAMTIME IN THE RAINBOW VALLEY

After thanking Croc and Heath for their advice we waved farewell to the Hughmongers. It rather tired us out, as for a relatively small town their numbers were humongous.
We soon reached the red rocks entrance into the Rainbow Valley, and it got real colourful from then on.

Red

Red animals abounded within the red of Rainbow Valley. Within the first hour I'd seen red kangaroos, red foxes, red-necked wallabies and redback spiders. Although we could see them clearly, and walked amongst them, no animals acknowledged our existence.
It was also red hot there, but the red river did not entice us to its banks.
Mars was the only celestial object visible in the sky, and it glowed brighter than I'd ever seen before; it was indeed a red planet.

Orange

The red turned to orange after a few miles, and the temperature cooled somewhat. I was all of a sudden reminded of Halloween, and the autumn/fall season. I saw no animals in orange, and instead it seemed to be full of fruit and vegetables.
The natural goodies included pumpkins, nectarines, mangoes, carrots, apricots; and of course, oranges. But even though they looked delicious, we didn't feel the desire to devour.

Yellow

Orange faded to yellow an hour or two later, and it felt as if we were inside a golden paradise. It was as if all the gold in the universe was spread out in front of us.

But even though the gold looked shiny and beautiful, we didn't feel tempted to extract it and weigh ourselves down; instead, we continued our walkabout.

Green

Sometime later; I was losing track of time to tell you the truth; the yellow turned green, as if mixed with blue. Memories of my Green surged through me. Our happy times together in the past lifted my mood, but then I thought of our current situation, and it made me lethargic.
Thick vegetation also made passage difficult, and tired me out further. I suggested a rest stop, and fell into a deep sleep soon after sitting down.

35. MEDITATIONS IN GREEN OF GREEN

My dream in green seemed to continue for an age, and I remember it vividly.

Meditations in Green to Animals Soundtrack

I didn't want to leave the comfort I felt in green, and the way it reminded me of Green, but I thought I could hear the song *We Just Gotta Get Out of this Place* again. I opened my eyes and saw that Bonzo and Elle had been joined around a bush telly by the *Animals* I dreamt about in Latham, Western Australia. I took the hint and rose from my slumber.
Between my decision and standing up, the *Animals* and telly disappeared, leaving just Bonzo and Elle sitting on the grass. They were very understanding about my time-out, saying it was nice to see me awake and refreshed. I didn't mention seeing the other stuff, as they might have thought I was losing it!
I certainly did feel refreshed, and it was as if my sleep had provided the green light to speed through Green. It wasn't long before I could see blue-ridged mountains in the distance. I remembered how Green and I passed through blue-ridged mountains on our North American ramble, meeting those two chaps searching for the lonesome pine.

Notes

Blue-ridged mountains feature in the song, *The Trail of the Lonesome Pine*, with Laurel and Hardy having sung a memorable version.
Meditations in Green is a book by Stephen Wright.

----

36. Blue on the Other Side of Green to Yellow

As we crossed from green forest to hills of blue
and the yellow completely faded from view
I encountered the poem, *Shropshire Lad,*
written by Alfred Edward Housman when sad.
I read it intently because I was
on *walkabout* in the land of Oz.
He also wrote of terrain with such a hue,
but while he longed to return to that view,
for me it was just another rainbow colour
on my journey to and fro, hither and dither.

Notes

Alfred Edward Housman and poem (*Shropshire Lad).*
Walkabout (Aussie film).

----

37. INDIGO BIRDS ARE INTUITIVE

We left the land of blue
without much further ado
I would like to tell you more
but fear the border was a bore.
Then off we did go
to the land of indigo
shown there by a dingo
who spoke our lingo.
'Goodbye!' We entered in one go
moving faster than slow
our expectations did grow
when we saw the land was low
so it was time to say 'Long so, hello!'
to our good guide, Dingo Joe.

Indigo Birds on Indigo Mushrooms

As we walked through a lea meadow filled with indigo plants,
two birds flew over our heads and landed on a couple of
lactarius indigo mushrooms. I noticed that both birds had
indigo plumage and three eyes.
As we approached their perches, one of the birds flung out its
wings and chirped, 'I am an indigo bunting called Ajna, and
this is my friend, an indigobird called Chakra VI. We would
like to welcome you to indigo. Our friends, we have been
watching you pass through, and we hope you have been
enjoying the indigo view. We believe you are looking for
Black Footed Rock Wally B.'
'Yes, that's right,' Elle replied, 'we were advised of that by
Croc Dundee.'
Chakra VI smiled, before singing to us: 'Yes, my friends, we
think you are nearing the meeting now. You will pass
through the land of indigo in peace, but this is not the setting
to encounter Wally B, that is as far as we can see. Please
enjoy the rest of your indigo journey.'
With that, both indigo birds flew high into the indigo sky,
and soon disappeared from view.

We did indeed continue through indigo in peace, and were soon walking amongst violet flowers that stretched for as far as the eye could see.

Notes

Ajna is the sixth chakra in Hindu tradition.

----

38. REACHING THE END OF THE RAINBOW

We knew violet was the seventh colour; the last of the rainbow, and our final chance to meet the Wally B key to our destiny.

Violet is Refreshing and Harmonious

We entered a haze, with light *Purple Rain* refreshing the senses after our time spent under the clear indigo skies. We heard some colourful electric guitar sounds lilting over the violet fields, and thought it might be Jimi Hendrix's *Purple Haze.*

So we followed the music to its source,
only to find it wasn't Hendrix verse,
or even anything slightly violet,
we were just thankful, it never fell silent.

Blackfoot Show Us the Way into South Australia

'*Good Morning,*' said the source of the music, 'I heard you've been *Searchin'* through the *Dry County*, and *Dream On* to *Fly Away*. My name is Black Footed Rock Wally B, and I hold the musical key to your Oz South destiny.'
Bonzo seemed amazed at Wally B's knowledge of us, and sang out, '*Let There Be Rock*!'
'Yes,' said Wally B, 'and *It's A Long Way to the Top* young Bonzo.' Wally reminded me of Gandalf talking to the hobbits when he said that.

Highway Song to the End of the Rainbow

I told Wally I'd expected to see MiMo Moby in *Blue*, and asked why he hadn't appeared. Wally explained that the magic of dreamtime in the Rainbow Valley was too strong for even good monotheists, so MiMo Moby could not have believed enough to enter.

Wally gave us a *Marauder* t-shirt each, which had an impressive eagle's head as the main image; saying he thought the t-shirts might be useful in Oz South. Then he said it was time for us to cross the border, and he knew a *Highway Song* to help us on our way.

I thought it must be the musical key Croc Dundee had talked about. We thanked Wally and let his song do its magic.

Notes

Dreamtime is an important part of Australian aborigine spirituality.

Blackfoot songs/album: *Good Morning, Searchin', Dry County, Dream On, Fly Away, Highway Song, Marauder*.

AC/DC songs: *Let There Be Rock, It's A Long Way to the Top*.

Prince song (*Purple Rain*).

Jimi Hendrix and song (*Purple Haze*).

Moby song (*Blue*).

Gandalf of *Lord of the Rings*.

----

39. SOUTH AUSTRALIA IN THE BACK OF A TRAILER

It did indeed do its magic, and we soon found ourselves on the edge of the Rainbow Valley, with normal colour resumed outside.

Understanding the Full Spectrum

We were met by Homer and Marge; welcoming us to the Simpson Desert. I looked back at the valley one last time, and it was nice to see a *Rainbow Rising* again.
It had been a great experience to be amongst all the colours and creatures for an extended period of time, and I thought I now had a deeper appreciation and understanding of the whole spectrum.

Simpson Desert, South Australia

Homer was driving a jeep, and Marge was in front with him, so we all jumped in the back. They hadn't brought the kids, so there was plenty of room. It was probably a good job they hadn't brought Santa's Little Helper, as Bonzo of course thinks it's a *Dog Eat Dog* world.
I thought it might be troublesome crossing the Simpson Desert with the *Simpsons*; but we travelled from delightful Birdsville, to challenging Mount Dare, without any problems. The Simpsons arranged for some friends to pick us up at Mount Dare, and they were there with their trailer when we arrived.
After introductions, we thanked the Simpsons and bade them farewell, before jumping in the back of the trailer. I really bonded with Wesgrey, a Western grey kangaroo; Elle got on well with Jane, a Lake Eyre dragon; and Bonzo had a dog's life with a barking owl called Barkatowt.
I had a good chat with Wesgrey about kangaroo mythology. He said their creation myth told of their escape from the Grapes of Rolf, and how they lived their lives fearing the return of Rolf.

Notes

Homer and Marge Simpson (cartoon couple, and their dog, Santa's Little Helper).
Rainbow album (*Rainbow Rising*).
Jane Eyre (novel by Charlotte Bronte).
Rolf Harris had a big hit in 1957 with an adaptation of an old Aussie folk song: *Tie Me Kangaroo Down, Sport.*
The Grapes of Wrath is a 1939 John Steinbeck novel about the American Great Depression.

---

40. OPAL THAT ESCAPED THE TRADE POINTS WAY TO ADELAIDE

We travelled west for what seemed like an age,
but it wasn't like we were trapped in a cage,
the vast distances of the outback stretched out,
and we were totally free to go walkabout.
It was also nice to just sit back and relax,
observe stars dancing on water to the max,
as we passed Lake Cadibarrawirracanna,
the second longest official name in Oztralia.

We continued travelling south at quite a pace in the wide open space, and reached Quorn around midday. We had a magnificent meat substitute lunch there. Wesgrey, Jane and Barkatowt were so full they were going to sleep it off; but we wanted to get going, so we bade them farewell and thanked them for the lift before continuing on foot and paw.

Lost and Found, Time Spins Around

We couldn't find the dust sandy path
and were going to visit Whyalla,
but we asked a few people directions,
and they didn't seem to have a clear answer.

We were a little lost, but then saw a giant greenygrey coloured opal which must have escaped the opal trade. It seemed to be pointing in a certain direction, and my hat was shining, so we followed it. Lo and behold, we soon arrived in Adelaide. However, just as I felt our luck was changing for the better, a sudden timequake sent us hurtling into another dimension.
As we span toward an alien ground, I saw we were about to land next to a stadium where there was a weird looking game taking place; like a mixture of Australian rules and cricket merging into football. One team seemed to consist of crows, and the other redbacks. After landing and recovering our

composure, we walked toward the stadium, meeting a cane toad along the way.

We approached the toad, and introduced ourselves. It reciprocated the pleasantries, introducing itself as Professor Theold Gumtree, expert in the field of timetravelicity. I told Theold about our *in the wrong place at the wrong time* predicament, and asked if he knew of a solution.

Gumtree thought for a moment, before saying, 'If you can guess the winner of the AusRuIcket game I will be able to return you to your time; but if you are wrong there will be a costly forfeit.'

Notes

AusRuIcket is probably inspired by J.K. Rowling's quidditch sport in the Harry Potter novels.

Quorn is a town in Australia and a meat-substitute vegetarian food company.

Adelaide Crows is an Australian Rules Football team. South Australia Redbacks is a cricket team.

----

41. FANTASY SPORT DECISIONS DECISIONS

We got in a huddle
and a bit of a muddle
working out a preamble
to finish our ramble.
I rubbed my hat
until it was flat
and then it shone:
a sign of game on?
The crows have two wings
talons and beak,
redbacks have eight legs
a fiery streak.
Who will win the contest
it is difficult to decide;
could be down to injury
or a contentious offside.
Choosing could be
a hat-trick calamity
for three travellers
trapped outside normality.

42. TIME TO THINK...

Time will make you Wait, and never be Late

Tick, tock, tick, tock,
time waits for nobody
even in a state of stagnancy
of an alien world strange city.
Crows can fly
redbacks scurry by
if they fought beyond Y
which one would die?
It's a dilemma, my oh my,
could easily induce a cry.
What temperature is ice meltable?
No, their choice is more hypothetical
than some real world conundrum
that is scientifically measurable.
We cannot help, or advise,
for our words would become lies
in a land where time waits for no-one
and only flies when it's having fun.

Had time stood still? It certainly seemed so, and I was none
the wiser. Then Elle looked up and pointed to the *Marauder*
t-shirts; before reminding us that Wally B had said he
thought they'd be useful in Oz South.
Tension was replaced by relief, as we looked at each other
with knowing grins. Elle confirmed my thoughts, 'Crows are
birds, and the *Marauder* t-shirt features a bird image, so
according to Wally B theory, the crows will win.'

We rushed over to Theold Gumtree
and said we'd wager our timesanity
on Crows to beat Redbacks
confident we'll make tracks
back to our own place in history...

43. MATCH OF THE DAY FOR FINDING OUR WAY

Wager laid, we rushed over to the pitch for the start of the game.

First Half is a Laugh... For a Redback Giraffe

After the game started, it was immediately plain to see, what a great spectacle it would be. There were thousands of Crows and Redbacks supporters cheering on their teams. The biggest contingent of Redbacks supporters seemed to be giraffes, while most Crows fans were llamas.

The Redbacks took an early lead when Redgrave buried the ball between the posts. They soon extended their lead through Reddin, inspiring a roar from the Redback end like nothing you've heard before. Just before half-time, *Redburn* seemed to fan the flames of our misfortune when it extended the Redbacks lead.

Grey Joins in with the Murder of Crows

I wondered if all was lost, but Bonzo thought he spotted a weakness in the Redbacks defence; suggesting they looked open to attack from above. He thought the Crows should use their aerial prowess, instead of trying to play it on the ground.

I saw the logic in Bonzo's strategy, but couldn't think of a way to put it into practise on the ground... and air! It was murder trying to formulate a plan for a collection of crows that looked rooted on the wrong side of a ruthless Redbacks streak.

The worry made me feel as sick as a parrot; but that negative was turned into a positive when it inspired me to remember my ability to shapeshift. I told the others I was off to join the Crows, before quickly changing into one. They wished me luck as I flapped for the field. Rather than feeling like a sick parrot, I now felt like I could fly over the moon. I hoped my elevated mood would lift the Crows, and once on the pitch:

I squawked my views on second-half play,
told them it was vital to our right of way,
before volunteering as Crow Grey,
to join the sporting fray.

They accepted my offer, and I lined up for the second-half.

Notes

A collection of crows is called a murder.

----

44. SECOND-HALF OF THE GAME IS NOT THE SAME...OR LAME

The whistle blew to start the half,
our attack was higher than any Redback giraffe.
A new urgency. Down the wing, on the wing;
you should have heard the Crow llamas sing:
We love Crows, We love Crows. Because,
we flew on a Mexican wave from Andes to Oz.

Russell Crow put in a perfectly flighted cross, Sheryl Crow
knocked it down for me on a sixpence, and I slotted it in. It
was a dream start to the second half, and we were back on
track. There was no time to crow about it though; we had a
game to win.
Twenty minutes later, Bob Crow pulled another one back
with a short snap strike, leaving the Redbacks defence red-
faced as well as red-backed.

Crows were back in the game, but it's a funny old name

But just as everything looked hunky dory
Ted Hughes Crow had to go off with poetry
Jim Crow divided the team like a tidal wave
Brandon Lee Crow tragically sent to early grave
and Charlie Crow had to fly off to trade.

Elle and Bonzo are the Ace and Joker in the Pack

We were now two players short, so I had a word with Bob,
and he called a time-out. I rushed over to Elle and Bonzo,
who were already on the edge of their seats.
I quickly taught them the skills of shapeshifting, and they got
the hang of it in no time. Elle Crow and Bonzo Crow joined
the fray without delay.
Bonzo made his presence known in no time, with some
crunching tackles in the middle of the park that were
reminiscent of Blackport's Nipper Lawrence in his prime. It

was from one of those that he won the ball, and then proceeded to dribble it past and through more legs than I could count, before slotting it straight under Redglove's outstretched leg for our equaliser.

A Thrilling Finish to the Game

It was 3-3 with ten minutes remaining, and everything to play for. Our timewager didn't include extra-time, so it was vital we found a winner before the end of rhyme.
But the Redbacks attacked straight from the kick-off, and moved the ball about so silkily that it looked as if it was stuck to their feet on a sticky web. They were soon inside our penalty area and threatening to score a winner of their own. However, our goalie, Crow Nation, flew up to the top corner and not only saved the shot but also gathered it in its outstretched wing. It quickly threw the ball the length of the field.
Elle was upfield and onto it like a natural bird. She reached the ball before the Redback full-back and sent it flying over the stranded Redglove to put us in the lead. It was a great use of her bird body, and the Crows fans flew into a state of euphoria.
There was hardly time to restart the game, and the final whistle gave us the Crows victory we needed.

Notes

Mexican wave is a crowd interaction that started at the 1986 World Cup in Mexico.
Andes - South American mountain range.
The Crows - Russell Crowe (actor). Sheryl Crow (singer). Bob Crow (union leader). Ted Hughes and poem (*Crow*).
Brandon Lee and film (*The Crow*). Charlie Crow sells clothes.
Blackport Rovers and Nipper Lawrence (football team and player in *Tiger* and *Roy of the Rovers* comics).
Crow Nation (Native Americans).

45. TIME TRAVELLING TRIO RETURN TO MODERN ADELAIDO

We commiserated with the Redbacks; they didn't seem too disheartened, and the players sportingly clapped us off using all eight legs.

Going Downhill after Victory

After celebrating with our Crow teammates we changed back into our normal shapes and headed over to where we remembered Theold Gumtree had been. We walked in a jubilant mood, and Elle said she was glad to be back in her usual body. I thought that was a good sign, although she had been a beautiful bird. Our unbridled joy was short-lived however, and was soon to be replaced by pesky puzzlement.

As we approached
the remembered location
we reached a slope
we couldn't recall,
and the decline was so steep
we began to fall.
We had to start running
to stay on our feet,
skidding and sliding
to an uneven beat.
I could stay upright no longer
and gave out a yell
as I fell
into Elle.
Then we both took out Angry,
and tumbled like puppets
all dingly and dangly.

Returning to Time

I thought we might not survive, such was the dive, but after a minute or three we began to slow down. Elle brought us to our final stop by grabbing us. I had to laugh when Bonzo turned around to me from under her right arm and declared: '*She's Got Balls!*'

We had landed back on the dust sandy path. After dusting myself off I had a good look around, and saw there was a memorial to The Old Gum Tree where we remembered meeting Theold Gumtree.

Notes

The Old Gum Tree is the historic site of the proclamation of the colony of South Australia in 1836.
She's Got Balls (AC/DC song).

---

46. KANGAROO ISLAND ROYAL RECEPTION

The dust sandy path led us out to Kangaroo Island. It didn't seem to be the logical direction, but we had faith in following the path.

Kingscote Little Penguins

We were welcomed by a right regal looking kangaroo called King Scote. He told us we should call him Scoty, and were his guests; so we would want for nothing while on the island. Scoty introduced us to a colony of little penguins that enjoyed the freedom of the land; he said they didn't take up much space because they are the smallest penguins in existence. They were very pleasant and playful, and struck up an instant rapport with Bonzo.
Bonzo relished telling them how he'd scored the third goal for the Crows in our epic AusRuIcket game. They said they'd love to learn how to play, so Bonzo started teaching them.

Time to Ramble

Scoty seemed to be a tad smitten with Elle, so when he offered to show us his realm I declined the offer, and said I'd like to do some solo rambling around the island.
I crossed Little Sahara and the Flinders Chase National Park, before relaxing in the wonderfully colourful and clean Vivonne Bay. I had a nice chat with a couple of pelicans called Viv and Yvonne there, before they left to get a bite to eat.
I fell asleep on the beach.

47. PARADISE SUNRISE WAKES GREY TO NEW DAY

Waking up in the sunrise haze
put me under a twilight daze
and I only remember it in poetry
so here's my V Bay second day story.
Waking on settled sands
with the sunrise hands
hugging sea and spray
in warmth across Vivonne Bay
I just wanted to lay
there all the day
before remembering time
Bonzo, Elle and other half Lime.
So I got up slowly
because I still felt lowly
if I'd gone for a swim
and water'd filled to brim
I wouldn't have felt wholly
because I've got a holey
or three in my head
to stop me feeling like lead
girl o boy I ain't no buoy
sometimes I'm coy or koi
carping on about all things fishy
and telling Green how I miss ye.

48. GREY MEETS THE ANGRY NEIGHBOURS ON RAMSAY STREET

I eventually hauled my sun-kissed furry ass
off the sun-soaked golden sandy mattress,
strolling away from my paradise resting place
I *wombled* along freely to leave no trace.

Meeting the *Neighbours*

As I left the beach, I turned around for one last look. Then I
headed into town. The first road I reached was *Ramsay
Street*. It looked like a nice neighbourhood, and there was a
wedding going on.
As I walked along minding my own business, one of the
Neighbours introduced himself as Harold Bishop. He said
they needed something to dull the wedding a little, as it was
too bright to take quality photos. I said I'd be happy to
oblige.

Grey in the Neighbours Wedding

So I joined the wedding, and thought I added a nice touch of
dullness to balance the light. Everybody said I did a grand
job, and the marrying couple, Charlene and Scott, invited me
for drinks afterwards.
After having a drink or three, I *Suddenly* got talking to a man
with a rose tattoo. His distinctive ink helped me recognise
him as the one who'd *Suddenly* burst into song at the
wedding. He introduced himself as Angry. I asked why he
was called that, and he said his *Neighbours Suddenly* started
saying he had no mind when he got tattoos, and it made him
angry.

Notes

The Wombles were environmentally friendly 1970s fictional
creatures created by Mike Batt.

Neighbours (Aussie soap opera) and characters (Harold Bishop, Charlene and Scott).
Rose Tattoo and singer, Angry Anderson.
Suddenly was an Angry Anderson solo song for the *Neighbours* wedding of Charlene and Scott.

----

49. ANGRY TALKS LYRICALLY WITH GREY - AGREES TO GO AWAY

I asked Angry if he enjoyed living on Ramsay Street. He said the *Neighbours* were usually quite nice, but he didn't feel like he fitted in that well. He'd seen a fight between the *Butcher and Fast Eddy* when he was young, and it made him into a *Rock n' Roll Outlaw*. He'd become *One of the Boys* in a rock n' roll band, and *Nice Boys* don't play rock n' roll, so he'd become a B*ad Boy for Love*. A guitarist called Pete had done well good supporting him on the slide, but then he'd had to leave, so Angry was recovering from another setback.
I suggested a *Remedy* for his situation was that he could come and *Tramp* with us.

Bonzer Bonzo

Angry said it sounded like a 'bonzer idea.'
I said it was my idea not Bonzo's.
Angry calmly pointed out that I'd misunderstood him; bonzer is Aussie slang for great.
I profoundly apologised, and was relieved that my misunderstanding did not change Angry's mind. I said no more.
We left Ramsay Street to rejoin the others.

Notes

bonzer – Aussie slang for great.
Pete Wells was a founder and (slide) guitarist in Rose Tattoo. He died in 2006.
Rose Tattoo songs: *Butcher and Fast Eddy, Rock n' Roll Outlaw, One of the Boys, Nice Boys, Bad Boy for Love, Remedy, Tramp.*
----

50. ANGRY'S DISCOGRAPHY ILLUMINOSITY

As we hiked back to the others we saw an *Assault and Battery*, and it inspired Angry to sing that it felt good to be *Out Of This Place*. But he later said he intended to heed *All The Lessons* he'd learnt; and as for any pent-up resentment, he'd just *Let It Go*.

Angry Assuaged, Bonzo Bagpiped

I said that was probably a good attitude, as otherwise he could be *Scarred For Life*. That inspired Angry to sing that he had a feeling *It's Gonna Work Itself Out*, and if we're not bothered *Who's Got The Cash, We Can't Be Beaten*.

Walk this way
Kingscote sway
me and Angry
rhythmically
down the beach
until out of reach
of the neighbours
and hard labours.

By the time we reached the outskirts of our destination I felt I knew Angry a lot better, and had become convinced that he'd be a great asset on our epic Ozyssey.
The first sound that reached our lugs on the approach to the King Scote realm was that of bagpipes, and when the player came into view I was shocked to see that it was none other than our Bonzo.

Notes

lug - slang for ear.
Rose Tattoo songs: *Assault and Battery, Out Of This Place, All The Lessons, Let It Go, Scarred For Life, It's Gonna Work Itself Out, Who's Got The Cash, We Can't Be Beaten*.

51. BONZO BANISHES BAGPIPES BAFFLEMENT

When Elle saw us arriving she ran to meet us. She said she'd been worried, and was glad to see me back in one piece. I replied that in Oz I was already only a half of one piece really, remembering my green other half, but I was indeed still in one half piece.

Elle chuckled, before saying, 'Well, if you're going to be pedantic, it's good to see all your Grey self again. I would love to meet your green other half one day, and see you all together as the Greenygrey, but I've only known you as Grey.'

'Thank you kind Elle,' I replied. 'I should have been more laissez-faire, and especially at this joyous moment, but I do miss my limey other half ever so much. I do dearly hope that one day you will meet me as one half of the complete Greenygrey.'

AusRuIcket and Bagpipe Racket

One of the little penguins recognised us and told Bonzo, who was still playing the bagpipes. Bonzo quickly lay them down and sprinted over exuberantly.

After we'd greeted each other, I asked Bonzo what all the noise was about. He said the little penguins had so enjoyed playing AusRuIcket that they'd presented the bagpipes to him. They'd also burnt another set of bagpipes, and would play an AusRuIcket tournament for them every year called the *ARIshes*.

I said that was great news, but where had the penguins found all the bagpipes. Bonzo said it was like me: a mysterious grey area that went back a long time. However, little penguin legend said a Rockhopper brought them over.

Notes

Rockhopper is a type of penguin.
Bon Scott played the bagpipes, and wrote an AC/DC song

called *Rocker* along with Angus and Malcolm Young.
Ashes (cricket trophy).

----

52. AB/DC IS BORN

I introduced Angry to everybody, and we had a fantastic feast that night. It was also our last night on Kangaroo Island, as we decided during the meal that we needed to get rambling again. We told our hosts.

AB/DC is Born

Angry fitted in well, and seemed to enjoy himself; even singing a few songs toward the end of the night. Bonzo played the bagpipes for one of Angry's songs, and Elle danced wildly to the jolly tune. Everybody and everything seemed entranced by the music and dancing, and especially ol' Scoty.

Elle later said she'd enjoyed the music so much that she hoped there would be more when we returned to the road. She thought Angry and Bonzo gelled so well together they should form a band, and suggested Angry Bonzo / Dandelion Cordial would be a good name. Everybody agreed it was a wonderful choice. Angry added that it could be called AB/DC for short, and everybody thought that was another great idea; and good use of Angry's mind. At the end of the night, Angry said he felt like we were:

Blood Brothers and Sisters
Slipping Away from the *City Blues*
on a *Once in a Lifetime* opportunity
with *Nothing to Lose.*

The music also made me feel creative, so I wrote a little ditty of my own before retiring to bed. And here it is:

With a musical spirit
I thought we'd make it
we had the body and mind
sung our troubles behind
more adventures to come
maybe somebody's gonna drum.

Notes

Rose Tattoo songs: *Blood Brothers, Slipping Away, City Blues, Once in a Lifetime, Nothing to Lose.*

---

53. ON THE ROAD AGAIN

King Scote and the little penguins were up early, and had prepared a farewell to friends breakfast buffet on the beach. It was most enjoyable, eating freshly cooked tasty treats as the sun rose. But,

like each day's sun,
each week's fun,
each month's moon,
each year's seasons,
and each life's spirit;
all that shines must wane.

We ate our fill shooting the breeze; it was a shame we had to leave. I had thoroughly enjoyed my time on the island, and felt no regret about staying longer than planned.

Skippy versus Rolf

Scoty said he was sorry to see us leave; his final words to us were: 'Goodbye my friends. May Skippy be with you, and you never meet the Rolf.'
The little penguins said it had been great to meet us all, and especially Bonzo; they would think of him every time they played AusRuIcket.
Then they all waved us off, and we waved back.

54. SEA STORM BEYOND PALE CORN

Four Sail For Sale

We set sail for the port of Robe
not far across Oz in terms of globe
as we'd heard there were bargains
in a supermarket without chagrins.

But waves did suddenly rise
in a storm of enormous size,
we wondered where it had brewed,
fury of the worst bad mood;
before it declared its intention,
to sink us without hesitation,
and leave no trace
of our boat race.

Notes

boat race - slang for face.

----

55. TAZ-MANIA IS A SAVIOUR AND STORM ABATER

Taz-tastic Treat for Two Times Two

For two days the storm did blow
waves and spray like driven snow,
we did our best to hold on tight
two to the left and brace to right.

Barracuda and tuna flew past
as if fleeing from a deep line cast,
I began to fear all was surely lost
seeing a storm from a distant coast,
approaching at an incredible speed
I thought *that's all we need.*

But it was the storm it repelled
and with giant waves quelled
the new spinning fury did land on deck,
and when it calmed above the neck
we could clearly see it was cartoon Taz
along with his friends, Baz and Caz.

Notes

Tazzy (cartoon character and show).

----

56. KING ISLAND HAS A SURPRISING AMOUNT OF INTEREST

Boatry Poetry is a Form of Libertree

Row, row, row the wave
surface of Davy Jones's grave
we could sit back and relax
as roaring forties cut us some slack
not trousers to wear
but no rowing despair
as the wind behaved as it should
you know they say 'well, it would'
sailing us towards Tasmania
I don't know how to explain to ya
we just sat back and played cards
as the boat ate up the salt yards
it wasn't long 'til we reached *King Island*
eating a Pearshape Egg Lagoon Currie by hand
shocked to see a Sea Elephant in Surprise Bay
but it was a fitting finale to a Bungaree day.

Notes

Pearshape, Egg Lagoon, Currie, Sea Elephant, Surprise Bay
and Bungaree are all King Island places. As are all the place
names in the next poem.
Davy Jones's Locker - sailor slang for sea.
Roaring Forties – strong westerly winds in the southern
hemisphere, especially between latitudes 40-49, which is
where Tasmania is situated.

----

57. POETRY VOYAGE WITH A SMILE BUT NO SAUSAGE

King Island to *Tasmania*

We tried to set sail from Disappointment Bay
but thunderous waves sent us astray
feeling like a ship of fools without a winner
we crashed into a smashing crag called Lavinia
moving us to the milky waters of Cowper Point
where the current took us to The Blowhole joint
we sheltered there for a little while
before getting blown the extra mile
for enough knots to reach Tasmania
landing somewhere near Marrawah.

58. TRAVELLING TASMANIA IS A FAWLTY FANTASIA

It looked rocky approaching Marrawah, which brought out a rousing rendition of *Let There be Rock* from AB/DC. I was worried about landing on the rocks, so I was relieved when Taz, Baz and Caz took us up in a perfect storm before setting us down safely on the Tasmanian terra-firma.

After partaking in a latte in Port Latta, we carried on to Penguin, where Bonzo brushed up on his Penguinese. They had a different dialect here to Kangaroo Island, but Bonzo could still make himself understood.

We then headed south over Cradle Mountain, which felt very comforting.

Arriving in Taz-mania is a Fawlty Fantasia

In fact, it was so comfy I dropped off to sleep.

When I awoke we had arrived in *Taz-mania*. Taz said he had a full house, but we could stay at the Hotel Tazmania, which was owned by his boss, Bushwhacker Bob.

He was a little grouchy,
but no *Basil Fawlty*,
Sybil must've been off her trolley,
Fawlty Towers was a folly,
even if *Manuel* was jolly,
and what about pretty Polly,
oh, don't get me reminiscy
about my time in *Torquay*.

After unpacking, we frequented the bar and met some of the locals. I got on great with Wendell T. Wolf, who was very friendly.

Notes

Bushwhacker Bob and Wendell T. Wolf are characters in *Tazzy*.

Fawlty Towers (1970s sitcom) and characters (*Basil Fawlty, Sybil, Manuel* and Polly).

----

59. IS TAZ-MANIA TAZORED TASMANIA?

Taz-mania in Seven Days for Ya

For one week we tasted Tazzy
from the basic to the snazzy
we met Taz's funtastic family
Hugh, Jean, Jake and Molly
Constance Koala kept us clean
and Dog the Turtle busy as a bean
Didgeri Dingo wasn't as much fun
and Willie Wombat has a lot to learn
but when it came time for us to leave
Taz had another surprise up his sleeve
presenting us with a ticket to Hobart
which gave our journey a great start.

Notes

Tazzy characters (Hugh, Jean, Jake, Molly, Constance Koala, Dog the Turtle, Didgeri Dingo, Willie Wombat).

----

60. HO BART IN HOBART IS NO ART

'Ho *Bart*! How's it going dude, haven't seen you for yonks; not since back in Springfield on the original ramble.'

Bart's Enjoying Hobart

We'd just arrived in *Hobart*, and I'd bumped into an old buddy of mine from the original epic Greenygrey ramble. As you know, we'd met up with his parents back in the Simpson Desert, but Bart hadn't been there.
Bart said he'd turned over a new leaf in Hobart, and was doing much better than on his family's visit to Australia; when he caused a diplomatic incident that ended up on television.
He said his parents told him about our meeting in the desert, and that they'd enjoyed our reunion.
I was introducing him to the others when he fired off a catapult at the *Tasmanian Tigers*, before throwing the catapult to me. I caught it instinctively; just as Bart told the Tigers I did it. Bart then ran off. I was left standing there with the catapult, not knowing what to do.
My mind was made up a few seconds later when the Tassie Tigers started running toward us. I legged it in the opposite direction, along with the others.
We were soon across the *Tasman Bridge* and scaling *Mount Wellington*.

Wild Horses and Tassie Tigers

There were wild horses on the peak, and Angry suggested we jump on and ride like the wind. I thought it was a good use of his mind. We rounded up four horses, and set off just in time, with the Tassie Tigers hot on our hooves.
The Tigers gave up the chase as we pulled away, letting out one last roar before disappearing back into extinction.

Notes

yonks – slang for a long time.
Bart Simpson, the son in the *Simpsons* cartoon family.
Tasmanian Tigers (surviving cricket team and extinct animal).

----

61. BEYOND THE LAND OF CHEESE, WOLFRAM IS KING

We thanked the horses for the lift, and raced north. I didn't know it at the time, but Hobart turned out to be the most southerly point of my Ozyssey.

Melton Mowbray is Cheesy Delicious

We reached Melton Mowbray in time for dinner/supper, and saw a sign advertising *The Scrumptioust Salubrious Surprise Supper Pie in South Oz*. We agreed it looked too good to miss, so we called into the food emporium advertising it.
The surprise turned out to be that there was only cheese included in the pie. It was still delicious, but we couldn't help thinking the advertising had been somewhat cheesy.

King Wolfram is a Grey Tonic

The dust sandy path took on a greyish appearance after Melton Mowbray. Angry told us it was because Wolfram was king here.
I thought it must be nonsense, and was shocked that something grey and wolfish could be king. Shock later turned to flabbergastation when I saw a piece of wolfram. Not only was it grey, but it also looked greeny in sunlight.

Notes

The Melton Mowbray in England is famous for food.
Central Tasmania has many wolfram (tungsten) mines.
----

62. CENTRAL TASMANIA PROVIDES PAINIER

Too Late to Pay Tribute to a Great

Wolfram showed us north
was the sensible way forth
over lakes of Great and Arthur
and across Central Plateau after
through Meander we did stroll
in Mole Creek we saw no troll
Jumpin' Jack Flash had a gas
with Angry Bonzo in Sassafras
from Beauty Point we did see a peach
Rebecca Fisher enjoying Green Beach
the vision swam gracefully out to sea
rising above waves until she was free.

Notes

Jumpin' Jack Flash (Rolling Stones song).
Rebecca Fisher (character in Aussie soap opera, *Home and Away*. She was mostly played by Belinda Emmett, who died in 2006).
----

63. GREEN BEACH IS BREACHED WITH DECORUM

We collapsed on the sand; fatigued by our rapid poetic journey through central Tasmania and shock loss upon reaching Green Beach.

We'd hoped the beach would be lusciously welcoming, but now it seemed devoid of spirit, and eerily silent.

Waves of woe
lapped the silent shore,
as we huddled without mirth
within a waning warmth.

Dec O' Rum Provides a Lift

Just when it was getting too grim for words, we heard a voice reach us from out at sea. It roared, 'Ahoy, me hearties, would you like a lift to the mainland. I'm on my way to Victoria, and I need a few more deck-hands on board for what looks like a difficult voyage.'

It seemed like great timing, and when my hat shone we agreed it was an irresistible offer. We swam out to the boat with renewed hope. We were helped on board by a rum-swigging sailor, and when I looked around the deck I saw that it was full of rum barrels.

However, despite all the rum on the deck and presumably inside the sailor, he still seemed to have a sense of decorum. So it wasn't a shock when he introduced himself as Captain Dec O' Rum.

64. DIONYSUS OF THE SEAS AND TIN KETTLE TEAS

We sailed up Bass Strait. I could hear a low thumping noise below the waves that sounded fishy.

Dai 'on the Seas' not Dionysus

I'd thought there was only Captain Dec O' Rum on board, but then he called down to somebody below deck. A few minutes later, a man emerged with a bottle of wine in each hand. His sleeves were rolled up, and shirt buttons undone; showing several female-image tattoos on his arms and chest.
'Hello butty,' he said to Captain Dec, 'anything I can do for you, like.'
Captain Dec replied that he wanted to introduce him to us. After telling him our names, Dec introduced the wine and women loving salty dog as Dai 'on the Seas'. We had a nice chat, and Dai said he had acquired his nickname to differentiate him from his two best friends back home, a pilot now known as Dai 'in the air' and a farmer called Dai 'of the land'.

Island Hopping

We stopped for a drink on Cape Barren Island, but it was completely dry. So we continued north to Tin Kettle Island, where we had a lovely home-brewed mug of Aussie tea.
It was getting late when we left, but Bonzo really wanted to visit Little Dog Island, so Dec said we could spend an hour or three there.
Bonzo had been barking up the right tree with his choice, as it was wonderful on the island; afterwards, I thought it was ruff luck we didn't also have time to visit Great Dog Island.

Sail Through Sister

As we sailed up the east coast of Flinders Island, Elle wanted to check out the Sister Islands. So we landed. The Sister

Islands Conservation Area was full of sisters, but Elle didn't recognise any.
We continued sailing north, and had a merry night singing sea shanties under the Southern Cross.

Notes

The Southern Cross is the most famous stars shape visible in the southern night sky. It is part of the Crux constellation. Dionysus was the Greek god of nature and wine.

----

65. PIRATES OF THE FOOTWEAR REGION

I slept well, and dreamt of a reunion with Green.

Yo Ho Ho and a Bottle Of Rum: *Treasure Island* Hum

I thought I could hear humming, and presumed it must be Dec, as the words I could make out were:

'*Fifteen men on a dead man's chest*
Yo ho ho and a bottle of rum.'

I remembered going to the premiere of the *Treasure Island* play as one half of the Greenygrey back at the start of the twentieth century, so it brought back fond memories.

Green Crocodile's Snappy Style

I thought I'd go and help Dec with whatever he was doing, but had a surprise when I ascended to the deck. Dec and Dai were nowhere to be seen.
That wasn't the only surprise awaiting me: there was something green navigating the ship. I thought it was my Green for a minute, after the dream I'd had, but soon realised it wasn't. When it turned around, I saw it was a crocodile. I was pretty sure Green wouldn't choose that shape for a reunion.
I greeted the green crocodile, and asked where Dai n' Dec were.
The crocodile stylishly snapped that they'd sold the ship to it during the night, before sailing off in another boat.

Pirate Lacost on Sail

I thought that was strange, as Dai n' Dec seemed to be looking forward to reaching Melbourne before we called it a night. Moreover, I couldn't remember another boat on board; just rum. I didn't mention that, and just introduced myself as Grey.

The crocodile shook my hand and introduced itself as Pirate Lacost, before climbing up onto the sail.

I was becoming ever more suspicious of it.

Notes

'*Fifteen men on a dead man's chest, Yo ho ho and a bottle of rum*' is from *Treasure Island*, a book by Robert Louis Stevenson.

Lacoste is a clothes and sportswear company.

Pirates of the Caribbean (film).

---

66. MOBY DICK MEMORY

I descended below deck to tell the others
the ship jolted violently before going overs
an eternity seemed to neverendingly pass
hurtling upside down in the strait of Bass.

The green crocodile rolled our ship
creating a nightmare morning trip
then it took us into a vertiginous dive
like a honey hunter digging into a hive.

It was looking for something but I knew not what
Captain Ahab hunted *Moby Dick* so I had a thought
that maybe Pirate Lacost was not what it seemed
but really 'Monotonous Monotheist' I screamed.
It emerged in bubbles, sound drowned in sea air
and maybe it was lucky, with panic not a good idea.

I swam back up to the top of the deck
wondering if I'd end up nervous on a shipwreck
and how could I survive a Davy Jones's locker fate
with a green crocodile snapping at my sea legs gait.

Notes

Captain Ahab is a character in Herman Melville's *Moby Dick*
book.

----

67. BATTLE BELOW BASS STRAIT STRETCHES CREDULITY

Deeper and deeper we did descends
down to the lair of the sharpest biting bends.

But the crocodile lost its glinting glare
as a ghostly apparition increased the scare.

My fear turned to joy as it became clear
the newcomer was nothing to beware.

It was MiMo Moby swimming our way
hopefully just in time to save the day.

The crocodile at once lost interest in us
as its nemesis joined the rumpus.

Then Elle shot out from below deck
and grabbed the crocodile's slippery neck.

They grappled amidst the ocean ripples
like drunken sailors after too many tipples.

And then I couldn't believe my eyes
as a green kingfisher showed enterprise.

It flapped its wings under the crocodile's thighs
making it change into a form we could recognise.

The two monotheists were together as if in sleep
as the mild dragged the monotonous farther deep.

We managed to control the ship's direction
navigating north to the sun's reflection.

Back on the surface I did jump with joy
as the kingfisher shapeshifted into the real McCoy.

It was my other half Green; reunited at last
we hugged so hard to the top of the mast.

68. GREEN AND GREY SEPARATE UNTIL ANOTHER DAY

Green and I were reunited once more into the Greenygrey; and Bonzo, Elle and Angry were excited to meet us together. When everything calmed down, we/I (Greenygrey!) cooked up a Bass Strait brunch for the whole bunch, and we discussed the previous day's exciting events.

Bonzo said he'd been asleep when all the excitement happened; he'd been that dog-tired! Elle said Angry'd suggested she rush up and grab our assailant around the neck. I thought it was a good use of Angry's mind, and Elle's body; they certainly seemed to be getting their confidence back in those areas.

We all hoped MiMo Moby would survive the deadly duel, and wondered if we would see him again on our journey. My hat seemed to glow when we talked about MiMo. Unfortunately, there was no sign of Dai n' Dec; we hoped they were safe somewhere.

Green for Pastures New

At the end of the meal we, Green and I, unfortunately had to announce that we would be parting again. The others were disappointed, but the Greenygrey world needed Green, and I thought I should conclude this quest on my own.

Green shapeshifted into an albatross for the long journey back to the Greenygrey world. We climbed to the top of the mast to wave it off, singing Vera Lynn's *'We'll meet again.'* As Green albatross reached the horizon it looked back, did a roll, and tipped its wings; before disappearing from view into the azure.

Notes

Vera Lynn and song (*We'll Meet Again*).
Ant n' Dec? (entertainers).

----

69. PORT FAIRY LOOKS MAGIC NOT TRAGIC

To the top of ocean sky
Green did seem to fly
higher and higher it did go
until I could see it no more.

We got back down to work thereafter
sailing the boat north with laughter
oh what joy to be alive on the seas
four friends travelling free as the breeze.

When Bonzo shouted land ahoy
the whole boat jumped for joy
and the first town wasn't scary
it was magical Port Fairy.

70. SYDNEY 2000 SPIRIT

As we approached the Port Fairy dock I saw a commotion in the sea,
and wondered what it could be.
Moments later, I realised it was MiMo still grappling with MoMo.

Ian Thorpe Swims to Save *Moby*

It looked as if MoMo had the upper hand, and was about to deliver MiMo the death-blow, when what looked like a human thorpedo sped through the water and delivered a hit to MoMo's underbelly.
MoMo flew into the air grimacing, looking out for the count, but managed to twist the other way before re-entering the water. I didn't see it after that.

Cathy Freeman, Spirit of Sydney 2000 Olympics

The thorpedo helped MiMo to the Port Fairy beach, and then a spirit runner took over. I had seen the runner training on the beach, showing spirit to continue when obviously somewhat dispirited, and then saw her run over to resuscitate MiMo.
After docking, we rushed over to them. MiMo said he was okay, although it had been a tough challenge restraining MoMo. The spirit introduced herself as Cathy.

Notes

Ian Thorpe (nicknamed 'Thorpedo' – Aussie swimming star of Sydney 2000).
Cathy Freeman (runner who lit the flame for the Sydney 2000 Olympics).

----

71. WEREWOLF POETRY AS TRAVELLERS LEAVE SHIRE

MiMo recovered well. Nursing MiMo also seemed to stimulate Cathy's spirit.
MiMo said he believed we'd won a major victory in our Ozyssey, and that we were now entering the final straight. That was good news, as I was already missing Green.
I thought Cathy would be a great asset to our team, so I asked her if she would join us. I was delighted that she agreed without much hesitation.

Leaving the Shire of Moyne

It was soon time to leave Port Fairy and say farewell to our mild friend. MiMo reminded me to stay aware, as more dangers lay ahead. He patted my head through the emerald cork hat as he said goodbye; my hat seemed to warm; before flying off in his porcelain pod.
MiMo's final words inspired another of my rambling poems, and I'd like to share it with you to bring the curtain down on this chapter:

We're Were Aware

Be aware where you are
Be a were wherever you are
Be a were and aware
Be aware you're a were.

Notes

Shire of Moyne sounds reminiscent of the *Lord of the Rings* shire.

----

72. ANGRY BONZO ROCK GEELONG WITH WERE SONG

We headed inland from Port Fairy as the sun rose to illuminate it; making the port and sea look magical. After that, we careered through Kirkstall; hurtled past Hawkesdale, and then sped down to Simpson. I thought our ol' friends the Simpsons might be there, but there was no sign of them. It was quite a relief that Bart wasn't there! Cathy upped the pace along the south coast, and her spirit seemed to rise a little with each step.

Maintaining speed to Torquay,
caused frazzled fatiguey
so we stopped for tea
at the hotel *Fawlty*.

The Fawlty reminded me of the Hotel Tazmania, which had reminded me of *Fawlty Towers*. The owner seemed quite confused when I asked for a Werewolf salad; not seeming to know how to make one. I told him it was similar to a Waldorf salad, and he seemed to remember making one of those before. We enjoyed the south coast snack.

Geelong is GGood for a Sing-Song

Our bellies full, we headed north-east to Geelong. The name 'Geelong' reminded me of Green and me when we are together, because our initials are a sort of long Gee: a GG. We called in a rock bar called Geelong Goodbye for dinner, as it advertised that Muse was playing there that night. We wolfed down a big meal in time for the band, but they didn't appear as scheduled. A couple of hours passed, with the crowd waiting patiently. Then it was announced that Muse had phoned saying they were being sucked into a *Supermassive Black Hole*, so they weren't going to be able to make it; they were sending their apologies as the line went dead.

I could relate to their predicament after my space flight over to Oz; I'd had a couple of near misses myself.

Angry said the band not turning up meant he wasn't going to be amused.

I was worried he was going to start raging, and asked him to remain cool if possible, but then he pointed out it was a joke: Muse, amused. I saw the funny side then and laughed... with a mixture of humour and relief.

It turned out to be a blessing in disguise in the end; Muse's cancellation, not Angry's joke; because Angry and Bonzo volunteered their services, and then played a tasty first performance as Angry Bonzo / Dandelion Cordial.

The crowd lapped up the bluesy rock beats, and one song was inspired by my recent werewolf poem. The chorus went something like this:

Beware of wereies?
Wereies cuss berries?
The most precocious of wereies?
No! Be cautious of berries.

When the Geelong Goodbye closed, we called in a nearby pub called the Duck and Drake for a nightcap.

Notes

Fawlty Towers was set in Torquay, England, and there is also a Torquay, Victoria; but it doesn't have a Fawlty as far as the author knows.

In *Fawlty Towers*'s *Waldorf Salad* episode (season 2/episode 3, 1979) Basil struggles to make a requested Waldorf salad.

Muse and song (*Supermassive Black Hole*).

Christopher McCandless died after eating berries while living in the wild; Jon Krakauer adapted his journal for the *Into the Wild* book.

---

73. MEETING THEE VB IS AN UNFORGETTABLE EXPERIENCEY

So Long Geelong, Thee VB Ode Memories

Waking up in Tin Can Alley
overlooking Metal Valley
I wondered where we were
the previous night a blur
Angry had a bruised head
Bonzo was painted red
Elle's hair was all a mess
Cathy looked like Queen Bess
I was lying across the yard
like an outdated discard
then Cathy recounted the night before
how we'd all danced around the floor
after meeting a fine Victorian beer
VB was our friend for life but not without fear
for it could taste so delicious on a hot day
that your mind and body would lose their way.

Notes

Tin Can Alley and Metal Valley are fictional. VB is real.

----

74. ANGRY GETS ANGRY

The Tale of the Duck-Billed Platypus Tail

Angry showed some sign of life;
feeling his head, he murmured
'Strewth, what strife!'

He looked over to us
with the eyes of a bruiser
and asked what occurred
in the Duck and Drake boozer.

Bonzo looked at him
with knowing eyes
and a dog-eared smile.

'Do you remember the platypus?'
Bonzo enquired,
as if already knowing the answer.

'No,' replied Angry
with a worried look
taking over his face.

'And the duck and drake?'
furthered Bonzo,
now certain of Angry's response.

'Not at all,'
was Angry's
predictable reply,
'I only remember entering.'

'Can somebody or something
please tell me what the heck
occurred last night,' Angry said angrily.

'Well,' said Bonzo,
'there was a platypus in the pub
last night, just enjoying a drink.'

Bonzo took a breath, and a sip of water,
taking his time to remember and recount the tale,
as I think he wanted to get it right the first time.

'And there was a duck working behind the bar.
They seemed to know each other,
and were getting along fine, until,
the duck gave the platypus its bill.'

'But what's that got to do with me?'
Angry exclaimed, sounding more
impatient than angry.

'Well,' continued Bonzo,
'The platypus went berserk
and started raging at the duck
that it must be quackers
if it thought all that had been drunk.'

'The platypus took a swing
with one of its otter feet
and when you saw that
you dived in and shouted 'duck'
to the duck. The platypus missed.'

'But the platypus steadied itself
before brandishing its beaver's tail
and before you had time to inhale
your head received the full flail.'

Angry looked astonished, and
asked Bonzo what happened next.

Bonzo paused, as if searching deep
into his mind.

Then he shrugged, and said
'Dunno mate, the drake
chucked me out.'

75. EASY RIDERS ON THE ROAD TO GILLIAN TAYLFORTH

We picked ourselves out of the gutter
without hardly a mutter,
but I did let loose a sigh,
as to Geelong Goodbye
we waved a long goodbye.

'Where do we go now?'
Bonzo asked somehow,
sounding like a fine wine
sweet *child o' mine.*

I said Melbourne was just north
and from this moment henceforth
we should call it Gillian Taylforth.

'Onwards to Gillian Taylforth then,
the time is already half past ten,'
cried Angry with zest n' zen.

A piper from the gate of lights
led us north to Hamlyn Heights
before a nice chap called Cornholio
showed us the way to Corio.

Lara gave us a lift to *Avalon*
where we joined the M1,
Cocoroc was a tasty aural treat
listening to music while you eat.

Notes

Gillian Taylforth (British actress).
The Piper at the Gates of Dawn was the first Pink Floyd
album.
Sweet Child O' Mine is a Guns N' Roses song.
Cornholio is a Beavis alter-ego in the *Beavis and Butthead*

cartoon.
Avalon is a *Lara Croft* film.

----

76. HOLLY VALANCE HALTS OUR ADVANCE WITH A GAME OF CHANCE

A frog fellow called Kermit Croaking helped us across Hoppers Crossing, before we got an easy ride with Dennis, Peter and Jack all the way to Gillian Taylforth. We said goodbye to the *Easy Riders* on the edge of the city, before continuing by foot and paw.

We went walkie
up to Niddrie,
perused Sunbury,
were told of hungry,
by a honey bee,
so we continued northerly.

Holly Valance's Bubble and Squeak Riddle at Riddells Creek

We were beyond peckish by the time we reached Riddells Creek; so we were delighted to see the Best and Scrumptious Bubble and Squeak stall on the side of the road.
We asked the woman at the stall how much it was for the fine looking fayre on offer. She replied:

My name is Holly Valance
and I'm going to give you a chance
to win all you can eat for free
by just answering a riddle or three.

Travelling Tribe Accept the Valance Challenge

I replied:

'We have faced many challenges on our journey,
so one or three more
is not as daunting a prospect
as it might have been a year ago.'

Holly Valance said that was great to hear,
and she was confident we would not err.

Then she revealed our Riddells Creek riddle, which had two
parts. Firstly, she asked us to name the city we had just been
in; and secondly, whether it was named such because Mel
Gibson was born there.

Bubble and Squeak Speak

We got in a huddle,
over a squeaky puddle,
ready to answer the Valance
knowing we could leave nothing to chance
for our bellies were starting to rumble
in need of a big brunch of bubble.

Notes

Easy Riders film and actors (Dennis Hopper, Peter Fonda
and Jack Nicholson).
Holly Valance (actress/singer).
Mel Gibson (actor).
----

77. BODY, MIND AND SPIRIT... AND BONZ THINK OF MELBOURNE

Tension
is no fun
when bubble
and squeak
free to dine
is on the line.

The Mind

We tried to think how the name Gillian Taylforth was
connected to Mel Gibson, but couldn't work out any
significant associations. Then Angry suggested the city might
have another name.
I thought that might not be as crazy as it first sounded.

The Spirit

I remembered then that I had indeed renamed it before we
arrived, but couldn't for the life of me recall another name
for it. I felt dejected, but then Cathy gave a pep talk to raise
our spirits, before offering to run back to the city to check the
name.
I had renewed hope.

The Body

Elle thanked Angry and Cathy, and said they'd done enough;
she'd like to make a contribution and check the city's name.
So Elle rushed back to the city, and when she returned she
said she'd seen a sign saying *Welcome to Melbourne*.
Yes, that was it; that was its name before I renamed it.

The Bonz

It had been an outstanding team effort; utilising body, mind
and spirit in the nick of time. I thanked them all. I wondered

if their efforts had also answered the second question, because Melbourne sounded like it could well have been named after Mel Gibson.

I put this to the team, hoping Angry would continue his good mind form. But before Angry could say a word, Bonzo piped up, 'Oh, Melbourne, that's easy, I grew up here. No, it wasn't named after Mel Gibson, it was after that pommie guy, William Lamb – 2nd Viscount Melbourne. Mel Gibson was in fact born in New York.'

We all looked at Bonzo in amazement, before giving him a big hug.

The Tucker

We gave the answers to Holly Valance, and she said:
'You had your chance
and now you can hanch
on my best and scrumptious
bubble and squeak.'

We tucked in.

Notes

William Lamb, the 2nd Viscount Melbourne, was Queen Victoria's first Prime-Minister, and lived between 1779-1848.
pommie – Aussie slang for a Briton.

----

78. A PASSER-BY UNDER THE LITERARY NONSENSE SKY

The fabulous five outback travellers
were sitting on the grass dividers
after eating their fill of bubble and squeak,
when a passer-by did unto them speak.

'I can tell you all you need to know
if you'll just open your door
I promise not to induce a snore
my presentation is not a bore
it's guaranteed to make you say cor!
and my jokes will raise many a haw-haw guffaw
it has not once started a war
or been considered against the law
all the donkeys have exclaimed e-oh
and most dogs have clapped at least one paw
the coldest ice maidens it did thaw
and even beavers stopped their gnaw
once I told it on the sea-shore
and the waves kept coming back for more
so what do you think my travelling four
are you ready for my rock n' roar?'

The passer-by looked at us
after ending the recital syllabus.

I said I thought he was mistaken,
because there was no door,
and we were five,
not four.

The passer-by looked all shocked and awe,
before declaring me a talking door.

'No,' said I,
'I've just eaten too much
bubble and squeak brunch,

and my body is now oblong.
So you are wrong; therefore, so long.'

79. RAILROAD SONG IN THE RAILWAY HOTEL, CASTLEMAINE BEER IN CASTLEMAINE

After the meal and passer-by had left us *dazed and confused*, we decided a drink or three was needed. So we headed up to Castlemaine and chose the Railway Hotel because it reminded us of Lynyrd Skynyrd's *Railroad Song*. We ordered six 4Xs for the five of us, because Angry wanted two.

The Code

It was a quiet afternoon, and our finking was frankly frazzled, so we lounged around watching a documentary called *The Code*.
It argued that there were numbers naturally embedded in nature, and that some numbers seem especially common and important.
I wondered if green and grey would be a top colour combination in a similar study on colours. I didn't say anything to the others because I thought it might sound supercilious; be treated as super silly, and not be taken super seriously.
We didn't overdo the beer this time, and all left the bar compos mentis.

Notes

finking – thinking.
4x is a Castlemaine brewery beer.
Dazed and Confused is a Led Zeppelin song.

----

80. NORTH VICTORIA FAST BLAST

Sizzling progress in the morning
eating up the miles from day's dawning.
Flat out for hours, apart from the sharp bends
by noon we'd reached Kangaroo Flat north ends.
Skipped straight through for a meeting at Eaglehawk
with a California Gully who liked to talk.
We wondered if Terrick Terrick,
was named after Terrence Malick?
Pyramid Hill pointed to Kow Swamp
where we were in need of a Wee Wee Rup,
and then it was north-west to Kerang
reminding us of a rock magazine called Kerrang.

Notes

Terrence Malick (film director).

----

81. GHOST DOG BONZO FINDS AC/DC BACK IN BLACK

There was a time-machine at the entrance to Kerang-Kerrang, and you could choose a decade to enter. The 1980s looked an exciting time, with the magazine-town being built and developed on a surge of metal euphoria. So we entered then.

Kerang-Kerrang Born too Late for Bon Scott

We had an eerie introduction to 1980s Kerang-Kerrang, walking through an arid barren region populated by just one gravestone. It reminded me of a scene out of a spaghetti western.

When we reached the gravestone I read out the inscription 'Ronald (Bon) Scott, born 1946, died 1980.' The next thing, Bonzo keeled over.

We revived Bonzo, and I asked if he knew what happened to him. He said he'd had a rush of déjà-vu when he saw the grave; as if it held some significance to his past. He'd felt an urge to dig into it, but had tried fighting it, and then his legs had given way beneath him.

AC/DC begin the *Kerrang* Construction

When Bonzo was steady on his paws we continued toward the first constructions in Kerang-Kerrang.

The first was a black house featuring a big mural of AC/DC's Angus Young on the front. I was admiring it with the others, until noticing Bonzo wasn't with us. I looked around, and poor Bonzo was on the ground again.

Bon Scott and Brian Johnson Meet

A man wearing a flat-cap emerged and exclaimed *Hell's Bells*. He introduced himself as Brian and asked what was wrong with Bonzo. We told him it was the second time it had happened today, and Bonzo'd said he'd had a sense of déjà-vu the first time. Brian said he'd go and get some food and drink. He returned with a beer and bone, and after reviving Bonzo told him to '*Have a Drink on Me,* and chew on this bone.'

Somebody shouted from the house asking him what he was doing, and he replied that he had *Given the Dog a Bone.* He then asked Bonzo if he could *Shake a Leg,* and when Bonzo showed he could, he invited us all into the house.

It was rocking in there, and a revitalised Bonzo soon became the life and soul of the party.

Bye-Bye Bonzo

Bonzo and the householders got on so well that they asked him to stay. Having recently remembered his upbringing in nearby Melbourne, Bonzo decided that he had found his place to settle.

We were all sad to be parting from Bonzo, but understood his reasons, and stayed until the morning to make a night of it. As we waved goodbye to Bonzo and the rest of them, they sang us off with: *You Shook Me All Night Long.*

Notes

Spaghetti westerns often have dramatic graveyard scenes, such as the concluding gunfight in *The Good, The Bad and The Ugly.*

AC/DC album and songs: *Back in Black, Have a Drink on Me, Given the Dog a Bone, Shake a Leg, You Shook Me All Night Long.*

----

82. TERMINATOR LIVENS UP KERANG-KERRANG

The four of us travelled farther into 1980s *Kerang-Kerrang*. We missed Bonzo, but knew the journey must continue.

Ale Hail Denim and Leather

The streets were full of people wearing denim and leather. The colourful patches sewn onto the backs of the denim supported a mix of traditional and new bands: Black Sabbath, Led Zeppelin and Rainbow were common names representing the former, while Saxon, Iron Maiden and Def Leppard were the most popular of the latter.

We strolled down Festivals Street, frequenting the Reading Rocks and Monsters of Rock bars; before moseying along Concert Alley and stopping off in the Bandwagon, Queens, Sophia, Marquee and Apollo.

Bonzo Catches Up with us in LA

Then we headed over to the LA district. As afternoon became evening we found ourselves on Sunset Boulevard. We were getting peckish, so headed over to the Rainbow Bar and Grill, where a promising band called Faster Pussycat was playing. We'd just polished off some veggie raindogs when Bonzo rushed in. It was a nice surprise and fantastic to see him, but it looked like something was amiss.

Bonzo said he'd remembered something from when he fainted that might be relevant to us: when he was unconscious he dreamt of a robot that would *Shoot to Thrill* trying to kill us. He couldn't remember anything else, so didn't know why or when.

We thanked him for his consideration, and started catching up with all our other news over a few drinks. A couple of hours later it was unfortunately time to say our goodbyes once again, and we all waved Bonzo *Back in Black*.

Grunge Terminator Shoots Down the Band

We had just finished discussing Bonzo's vision, and were asking each other why we hadn't heard more of Faster Pussycat in rock history, when I noticed a lone grungeman walk in looking like something out of another time. The next thing, he started shooting at the band, and didn't take long to turn it into a *House of Pain*.

Then he looked around to where we were sitting and took aim at us. Just when I thought we'd met our Waterloo, Dizzy Reed suddenly jumped into the space between us and starting shooting out *November Rain* from his portable keyboard.

The '90s trash metal classic startled the grungeman, and that gave Dizzy enough time to usher us out the back. We emerged into an alley, and for the moment at least, made good our escape. I had a momentary sense of relief, but it was tempered by the nagging thought: *What the hell is going on*!

Notes

Grunge music emerged out of Washington state in the late 1980s, and went global in the early 1990s.

Trash metal emerged out of LA in the 1980s, mixing metal, punk and glam. It was later lumped in with 'hair metal'.

The Battle of Waterloo in 1815 was Emperor Napoleon's last battle.

Bands, concert halls and festivals explained within the narrative.

House of Pain is a Faster Pussycat song.

November Rain is a Guns N' Roses song.

Dizzy Reed is the Guns N' Roses keyboardist.

----

83. WILL GRUNGE ROCK ROBOT DESTROY TRASH METAL MUSIC?

We sped through the alley, before ducking behind a *Uriah Heep* piled high in a derelict building carved out of rock. I blended in well with the grey surroundings, but the others were too colourful to be camouflaged. As we caught our breath in the net of time, I asked Dizzy what on earth was going on.

No Place for Trash in the Grunge Decade

Dizzy said that while there had been a peaceful transition from *trash metal* to *grunge rock* in the real world; in the media world where Kerrang resides, conflict had built up. As the 1990s wore on, and grunge lost its strength, a small group of grungementalists wrote their own history of the decade.

They believed that Kurt Cobain would not have left them if trash metal hadn't survived into the 1990s and made him miserable.

Of course, in reality Cobain had a lifetime of complex mental health issues, but the grungementalists didn't want facts to cloud their agenda, so they focused on only one or two episodes in Kurt's life.

The Making of Jeremy Grunginator

A shadow appeared at the building's entrance, and we readied ourselves for more death-defying excitement; but it turned out to be an old hobo who looked seasick the way he played his guitar.

Recovering from the scare, I took the opportunity to grill Dizzy some more, asking what the grungementalists had to do with our current predicament. He explained that they were led by a technological genius named Frank Grungenstein. Grungenstein supplied constant espressos in a secret coffee house, so his team worked all hours blending a

Pearl Jam with a Percolator. On the tenth attempt they perfected the Instant Prosecutor Ten.
I was already amazed, but there was more.
Dizzy said the IP10 was made *Alive* with electricity, and because it had an amazingly *Even Flow* it was nicknamed *Jeremy*. Its scientific name was the Grunginator. They sent it back to 1980s Kerang-Kerrang to destroy trash metal, in the belief that the 1990s would then be a better decade for Cobain and them, and grunge would remain strong.
It all made sense now.

Notes

Uriah Heep are a rock band named after a Dickens character in *David Copperfield*.
Kurt Cobain was the singer in Nirvana.
The old hobo is Seasick Steve (musician).
Mary Shelley's *Frankenstein*.
The Terminator (film).
Pearl Jam album and songs: *Ten, Alive, Even Flow, Jeremy*.

----

84. LOVE/HATE ARE WASTED, AND THE TARGET IS REVEALED

The seasick looking guitarist passed us and walked half way down the alley. He had just started singing that *you can't teach an old dog new tricks*, and that he had been *born with nothing and still had most of it left*, when he was sent flying back past us by a gunshot to the stomach. My shock was compounded moments later when I heard a voice say, 'We don't want no old trash in the future.'
Even Dizzy looked surprised. He whispered that he thought the Grunginator was out of control, as it was only programmed to kill trash metal bands; before saying we'd better scarper. So we raced down another alley in the opposite direction, and into a red room.

Meeting Love/Hate suffering a Blackout in the Red Room

Some musicians were suffering a *Blackout in the Red Room*; the room had an American decor, so it was obviously Love/Hate. It wasn't hard to recognise them, as they were famous for getting *Wasted in America*. We tried to warn them about the Grunginator, but couldn't awaken them.
A shadow at the door looked ominously like the Grunginator, so we continued running in the other direction, leaving Love/Hate to their fate. A few moments later, we heard several shots ring out in the room we'd just left. I guessed Love/Hate had once again been *Wasted*.

Angry Revealed as Target

As we ran down the corridor I glimpsed a billboard poster on the wall. It drew my attention because Angry was featured on it. The poster advertised Angry making a special guest appearance with Guns N' Roses at the Whiskey a Go-Go. The date had been scratched off, so I asked Dizzy when it was supposed to be happening.

After a few seconds of thought he said, 'Of course, that's it, tonight's the night when Angry inspires the LA metallers; propelling them into the 1990s. It's the Guns N' Roses concert with Angry guesting that the Grunginator is programmed to target. We've got to escape the Grunginator and get Angry to the concert somehow, or it'll be all over for trash metal.'

Wow, I thought, *our Angry is a rock n' roll star.*

Notes

Seasick Steve songs: *Started Out With Nothing, You Can't Teach An Old Dogs New Tricks.*
Love/Hate songs: *Blackout in the Red Room, Wasted in America.*

----

85. BRITISH HEAVY METAL AND ROCK AROUND THE BLOCK

We emerged into the neon streets of night-time LA. As we reached a roundabout, a Ratt jumped *Out of the Cellar* of a nearby building. It ran past us before going *Round and Round* in circles. We continued running, with the Grunginator hot on our heels.

British Rock in the Late 1980s

We entered the British quarter at the end of the 1980s. It had become a little run down by then, with hardly any new construction to add to the building blocks that had emerged in the early eighties classic period.

There was a small pocket of rising activity involving a *Cult* of *Little Angels* that had *Wildhearts* of *Thunder* worshipping *Dogs D'Amour*; but I heard gunfire after we passed through, so I feared the Grunginator might have destroyed the Temple of the Dog.

Return to the 1970s

Dizzy shouted that he knew a short-cut into the 1970s, so we followed him through some Doors to a *Moonlight Drive*, and after passing the *Roadhouse Blues* we arrived at *Venice Beach*.

Notes

Ratt album and songs: *Out of the Cellar, Round and Round.* 1980s British bands: Cult, Little Angels, Wildhearts, Thunder and Dogs D'Amour. 'Temple of the Dog' is a lyric in the Mother Love Bone song: *Man of Golden Words.* Doors songs: *Moonlight Drive, Roadhouse Blues. Venice Beach* in LA was where the Doors began. The *Italian Job* is a 1969 film.

86. DOORS AND BEATLES PLAY LIVE IN THE ITALIAN JOB

The 1970s were before Kerang-Kerrang was built, which was probably why it had such a surreal psychedelic atmosphere. Graveyardish backstreets reminiscent of Black Sabbath's early album covers crossed gaudy technicolor main streets that exiles from the 1960s would have rolled right into without noticing a stone unturned.

Doors of the Italian Job

We thought we'd lost the Grunginator, and strolled through the 1970s as if California Dreamin' on a winter's day; until a shot shattered my subconscious slumber. I turned around and saw the Grunginator hot on our tails.
We ducked into a hip looking jive dive by the name of *The Italian Job*. The Doors were on stage playing *Strange Days*, and I could relate to the sentiment of the song!

Doors to the Beatles

We found an empty table in a candlelit corner. Jim Morrison started singing *My Eyes Have Seen You*, which made me paranoid. I blew out the candle, hoping the Grunginator wouldn't see us if it entered. I felt more at home when the Doors ended their set with *The Changeling*.
The Beatles took to the stage after the Doors. I hoped they would *Help* my mood, but just after they started playing *I'll Get You* the Grunginator entered.

Notes

Rolling Stones album: *Exile on Main Street*.
California Dreamin' is a Mamas and Papas song.
Doors and Beatles songs explained within the narrative.

----

87. CHARLIE CROKER IN ITALIAN JOB AFTER THE DOORS

The Grunginator walked up to the bar and talked with a poison-dart-frog barman wearing a t-shirt with Charlie emblazoned on the front. The writing looked like it had been transferred onto the material from a PDF document. Charlie changed colours faster than my quickest chameleon.

At times Charlie was greenygrey,
but I certainly didn't know,
if that was its real display,
or if it was just for show.

Charlie Croker in *The Italian Job*

As the Beatles struck the first chords of *From Me To You*, I could hear Charlie croaking something to the Grunginator, but couldn't make out what he said.
They continued crok n' crowing throughout the Beatles and Rolling Stones shows. The Stones's set had several songs I related to in our current predicament, such as *19th Nervous Breakdown*, *Emotional Rescue* and *Gimme Shelter*.

The Grunginator Acts During the Encore

The Stones finished their set with *Let it Bleed*, and then the Beatles and Doors joined them on stage for an encore of *Rip This Joint*.
It seemed to trigger a reaction in the Grunginator, and it suddenly started shooting up the place after the first chorus; it didn't take long to finish off all the musicians on stage. Charlie Croker didn't seem happy about it at all, and I think the words he shouted afterwards will always haunt me.

Notes

Poison-dart-frogs are real and very colourful.
Charlie Croker is Michael Caine's character in *The Italian Job*.
Beatles and Rolling Stones songs explained within the narrative.

----

88. SURVIVING THE 1970S WITH THE HELP OF JIMI AND JANIS

Charlie Croker bellow-croaked: 'You were only supposed to blow the *Beatles Doors* off, I'm quite fond of the Stones!' Then he started shooting poison darts at the Grunginator like PDF files printed from a high-range printer. But the Grunginator simply opened its lid and percolated them. Dizzy shouted to us, 'We'd better getta bloomin' move on, it's time for a bit of self-preservation.' We legged it out the back.

Jimi Hendrix and Janis Joplin Help Us Escape the 1970s

We had trouble making our way across the *Crosstown Traffic* until a *Wild Thing* shouted *Hey Joe*, and then showed us the way to *Freedom, All Along the Watchtower*. He was heading to the *Valley of Neptune*, and wished us luck.

We walked a couple of blocks, and were getting lost again, until *A Woman Left Lonely* by *Bobby McGee* picked us up in a *Mercedes-Benz*. After telling us her story she asked where we wanted to go. Dizzy asked to be dropped off on the corner of the 1970s and 1980s. We thanked her before she drove off into *Summer*.

Grunginator is Alive and Well

I was just starting to relax again when I heard a flurry of gunfire. We ducked down while looking around, and saw the Grunginator hopping down the street a couple of blocks away. We looked at each other, and shared a *not again!* expression.

We started running in the other direction. Dizzy informed us that the Grunginator was programmed to incorporate any new skills it encountered. I had a primary example of that a minute later, when a poison dart whizzed past my left lug.

Dizzy said we'd better skedaddle back to the 1980s pronto, so we did. It was a relief to be back in the eighties, even though our futures were still hanging by a grungy doc marten lace.

Notes

Italian Job quote (*You're only supposed to blow the bloody doors off!)* and song *(Get a Bloomin' Move On [The Self Preservation Society])*.
Jimi Hendrix songs and album: *Crosstown Traffic, Wild Thing, Hey Joe, Freedom, All Along the Watchtower, Valley of Neptune.*
Janis Joplin songs: *A Woman Left Lonely, Bobby McGee, Mercedes-Benz, Summer.*
Hanging by a thread is a common idiom describing: chances running out.
Doc marten boots were a part of the grunge fashion that grew out of the music; although the fashion was not usually endorsed by the original grunge musicians.

----

89. ANDREW WOOD AND THE TEMPLE OF THE DOG

We re-entered the British Quarter, but couldn't lose the Grunginator, and it seemed to be gaining. Its newly discovered hopping technique made it look a lot quicker and scarier than when it relied on its old robotic movement. It also seemed to be creating and distributing more poison darts per-minute, and one was surely to hit the target before long.

Temple of the Dog Brings Out Spirit, Mind and Body

We were passing the Temple of the Dog, which was damaged but still standing, when Cathy sensed a spirit there. I hoped it was another sign of Cathy returning to her peak spirit level. I suggested trying to reach Andrew Wood, as he'd sung about a temple of the dog with Mother Love Bone, and might be able to reason with the Grunginator.

Angry pointed out that Wood became famous in Seattle rather than Britain, but said it was worth a try. I thought it was a good use of Angry's mind, showing knowledge and diplomacy.

Meanwhile, Elle was protecting us from the poison darts with her body. This was an incredible use of her body, and she certainly seemed to be getting her confidence back.

Dizzy Reaches Spirit of Wood with a Keyboard Tune

Dizzy unpacked his portable keyboard to play Mother Love Bone tunes he thought might tempt the spirit of Wood into our time and place in Kerang-*Kerrang*. He started with a great version of *This is Shangri-la*, but there was no movement around the temple. *Stardog Champion* was next, and my hopes rose with the mist swirling out of the temple base during the second half of the song. Was this the beginning of something special? It gathered pace, and soon the temple was hardly visible.

Eureka, as Dizzy finished off *Man of Golden Words,* the spirit of Andrew Wood appeared above the Temple of the Dog.

Notes

Andrew Wood was the lead singer of Mother Love Bone. He died in 1990.
Mother Love Bone songs explained within the narrative.

----

90. ANDREW WOOD CONVERTS TERMINATOR TO BLADE RUNNER

Andrew Wood looked at us, and then farther down the cobbled criss-crossed streets, where the Grunginator was fast approaching. Wood motioned us behind the temple, before putting his right arm up in the air while singing to the advancing robot: 'Stop right there *Captain Hi-Top*, because this has gone on long enough, you ain't been programmed right, and you need to tighten up your screws.'

Axl Rose not to Blame for *Kurt Cobain*'s Death

The Grunginator stopped, and seemed to show emotion for the first time. Did a tear roll down from its lid, or was it percolator perspiration? It was hard to tell through the swirling mists enveloping the Temple of the Dog.
The Grunginator looked up at Wood, saying 'I know you are a friend, as all the Seattle music heroes have been installed in my memory. But I know not what I do, only what Frank Grungenstein programmed in me.'
Wood looked down with sympathy, before telling it, 'I can see your *Heartshine*, but they programmed you with biased and incomplete information, blaming Axl Rose for Kurt Cobain's early death, and sending you back to the 1980s to eliminate him. Just look at me and my life; I never had no beef with Rose, but I also died tragically young.'

Terminator to *Blade Runner*

With that, the Grunginator seemed to calm down, and called for a time-out coffee break. It made a couple of cappuccinos for itself and Wood and they sat down on the temple steps.
It all seemed to be calming down, but then Alice in Chains fell out of the sky, singing *Down In A Hole*. Alice looked doomed, but the Grunginator reached out its handles and caught them.
The Grunginator looked into the eyes of Alice, before saying:
'I've seen things you people wouldn't believe: Faster Pussycat

screeching on stage at the Rainbow Bar and Grill; I've watched Seasick Steve die in a dark shared with Love/Hate. A poison-dart-frog glowing in the *Italian Job*; Janis and Jimi running wild in the 1970s streets. All those moments will be lost in time, like tears in rain. Time to fly.'
And with that it released Alice's chains, and Alice flew over the *Sea of Sorrow* to Nirvana.

Notes

The Grunginator speech is a pastiche of one in the *Blade Runner* film. In *Blade Runner*, the replicant Roy Batty delivered the following soliloquy after saving the hero, who was its previous target: 'I've seen things you people wouldn't believe: Attack ships on fire off the shoulder of Orion; I've watched C-beams glitter in the dark near the Tannhauser Gate. All those moments will be lost in time, like tears in rain. Time to die.'
Captain Hi-Top and *Heartshine* are Mother Love Bone songs.
Axl Rose is the singer in Guns N' Roses. He and Kurt Cobain didn't get along.
Alice in Chains and songs: *Down In A Hole, Sea of Sorrow*.

----

91. NO REST FOR THE LICKED: IT'S ALL GO, TO WHISKEY A GO-GO

We turned the corner of the Temple of the Dog, just as the spirit of Andrew Wood *Thru Fade Away* with a *Gentle Groove.* We could see no sign of the Grunginator, just a *Man In The Box.*

Remembering Angry's Appearance at the *Whiskey a Go-Go*

I was feeling drained, plum knackered in fact, so I lay down on the temple steps. I was about to drop off, when I heard Dizzy exclaim:

'I'm waking you up
before to sleep you go-go,
there's no time to rest
so Wham is a necessary pest,
Angry was supposed to be on floor
of the Whiskey a Go-Go
over an hour ago.'

It had completely slipped my mind, and seemed *Rock of Ages* since I'd seen the Whiskey a Go-Go poster advertising Angry's appearance.

Rushing Angry to the Whiskey a Go-Go

We rushed back to the 1980s, and arrived at the Whiskey a Go-Go in next to no-no time, pronto.
The crowd roared raucously as Angry took to the stage. The show went brilliantly, and Angry surprised us all at the end when he magicked a puppy out of his boot, telling the crowd it was a gift from the Temple of the Dog. I didn't see Angry receive it; maybe I did drop off before Dizzy's wake-up call. Angry left the stage to resounding cheers, surely having fulfilled his destiny to inspire the LA metallers.

It had been hard work, and downright dangerous at times, but it was rewarding to think we'd played a small part in saving trash metal.

Notes

Angry's puppy was inspired by a Zemanta photo of Angry Anderson holding a puppy.
Mother Love Bone songs: *Thru Fade Away, Gentle Groove.*
Alice in Chains and song: *Man In The Box.*
Wham and song: *Wake Me Up Before You Go-Go.*
Rock of Ages is a musical.

----

92. OZZY OSBOURNE'S BLIZZARD OF OZZ

As we emerged out of the *Whiskey a Go-Go* I saw a cloaked figure acting suspiciously in the shadows. The next thing, it was barking at the moon, and I became more than a tad worried. Was it some kind of lone-human werewolf?

Ozzy Osbourne's Blizzard of Ozz

Less than a minute later I felt a chilly wind on my back as a blizzard blew up out of nowhere. The shadowy figure shouted that Oz was no place for a dog, and he was going to take it to Ozz, which had 33.33% more room because of the extra z. I realised it was the 1980s Ozzy Osbourne. With his reputation for biting the heads off creatures I thought Angry's dog might be in great peril.

Elle Uses Her Body to Great Effect

My concern seemed justified when Ozzy sprang out of the shadows singing *Steal Away (The Night)*. Angry was still buzzing from his performance and seemed oblivious to Ozzy's overshadowing omnipotent obtrusiveness.
Ozzy looked certain to reach Angry's dog and snatch it away to a cold dog's life in Blizzardy Ozz, until Elle stuck out a leg and tripped him up. A *Crazy Train* was passing through town on the way to the 1990s, and Elle quickly threw Ozzy on board. I thought it was a great use of her body.
Ozzy seemed impressed as well, and shouted to Elle that it wasn't too late to join him. Elle responded with a 'No thanks!' This prompted Ozzy to sing *Goodbye to Romance*. I felt sorry for him then, but he seemed to have recovered before disappearing from earshot, as the last thing I heard him sing was, *No More Tears*.

Notes

Ozzy Osbourne and solo band name/album, songs: Blizzard of Ozz, *Steal Away (The Night), Crazy Train, Goodbye to Romance, No More Tears.*

----

93. PROG ROCK HELPS TRAVELLERS TO A GOOD SPIRIT SLEEP

I heard a voice announce there would be another *Crazy Train* in an hour. Although I was ready to leave Kerang-Kerrang I didn't really fancy that, so I asked the others if they had any ideas about how to move on with our minds intact.

Cathy Gets into the Spirit of it

Cathy said she thought she could feel the Wemba-Wemba spirit in the area, and if she could get a deeper contact she might be able to find a dream path.

I thought for a minute or three,
awaiting a perfect eddy,
to make me look brainy.
I was still paddling the surf ,
with the sea much to rough,
when Cathy said Prog Rock was enough.
I'd heard before it is the ultimate unwind,
so I left the stormy waters of my mind behind,
and agreed with Cathy on what to find.

Pink Floyd too Exciting for a Good Sleep

So off we rambled to find Prog Rock. It turned out to be easier than I thought, as a pig was flying above. A long *Wall* extended from Prog Rock to the *Dark Side of the Moon*, and herds of *Animals* seemed to be using it as a bridge between the two.
I suggested continuing to the ELPYesendless Lea suburb; because from what I knew, it was constructed for comfort and rolled on forever. It sounded perfect for inducing a good sleep.

Sound Spirit Sleep

So, under an ELP *Black Moon* on *Love Beach* we took our places *In the Hot Seat*. And Yes, *Close to the Edge,* holding hands in *Union,* we swept into slept until we could *Fly From Here*. It was like no other flight I'd experienced.

Notes

Prog(ressive) Rock is a complex form of music usually involving long instrument-orientated songs.
Wemba-Wemba is an aborigine group of people.
Pink Floyd albums: *Wall, Dark Side of the Moon, Animals*.
Pink Floyd had a flying inflatable pig in their stage show.
ELP (Emerson, Lake and Palmer) and albums: *Black Moon, Love Beach, In the Hot Seat*.
Yes and albums: *Close to the Edge, Union, Fly From Here*.
----

94. PERISHERS PREVENT PERISHING COLD IN PERISHER VALLEY

I awoke adrift in a snow drift. As I came to terms with my consciousness, and remembered the events in Kerang-Kerrang, I could see there were awesome peaks all around us. Climbing clear of the hole I'd made for myself, I saw Cathy and Elle were kindling a fire, while Angry was building a snowman.

I helped Angry finish off the snowman, and then we joined Cathy and Elle as they cooked up some wild vegetable broth. I asked if anybody knew where we were. Cathy said it was the Perisher Valley, in the Snowy Mountains of New South Wales. We had crossed over the state border during the dream.

Perishers Peruse our Parky Party

I had just about absorbed Cathy's geographical information, when some interesting characters wandered out of the nearby forest pushing a pram and pulling a wooden buggy. They were heading our way.

I said howdy when they got within earshot, and asked where they were heading.

The one pulling a buggy said they were on their annual holiday from the *Daily Mirror's Perishers* cartoon, and were making their way home to Crunge after getting ejected from the train again.

He introduced himself as Wellington, and the other humans as Maisie, Marlon and Baby Grumpling. The Old English Sheepdog was called Boot.

Perishers Save Us from Perish the Thought

Elle asked them if they'd seen any dead wood on their travels, as we were running out, and there might not be enough to finish cooking our food. Marlon said they hadn't, but he offered us his buggy, saying it wasn't one of his most genius contraptions, and hadn't been much use in the snow.

We were overwhelmed by his generosity, and thanked him profusely before quickly dismantling it and heaping it on our *bush telly*.

Notes

The Perishers story and characters explained within the narrative. Marlon was known for his genius contraptions.

----

95. ANGRY'S ADOPTION OFFER

The veg broth was cooking well, and everything seemed swell.

Angry's Dog Gets the Boot

Angry's dog was getting on with Boot like a house on fire; warming the cockles of my heart in front of our flaming bush telly. I hadn't seen two critters take to each other so quickly since *Grizzly Bear Adams* met *Ben*. The dog duo seemed inseparable by the time Marlon said the *Perishers* had to leave. I felt sorry for them, until Angry said it looked like his dog had found a new home, and told the *Perishers* and Boot to look after it.

Angry's dog looked sad as we said goodbye, but walked proudly beside Boot at the head of the gang as they left.

Beware Smiggin Holes

Before leaving, Maisie warned us to beware of Smiggin Holes if we were heading east, as there was some weird poo going on down there. Her warning sent a shiver down my spine; well, it was either that or the cold; as that was the direction I could see the dust sandy path leading.

Boot's new best friend barked a final goodbye before disappearing from view, and Angry led us in shouting and barking our farewells.

Notes

Grizzly Bear Adams was a television series about a wilderness man called Adams who saved and befriended a grizzly bear he named Ben.

----

96. WIZARD OF OZ METAMORPHOSIS INTO LORD OF THE RINGS

After eating our fill of veggie broth we had a good night's kip snuggled up in a huddle under a puddle sky. We packed up and cleared away in the morning, before following the dust sandy path in the direction of Smiggin Holes. The path was as much powder snowy as dust sandy now.

Smiggin Holes Strange Happenings

As we entered the forested valley on the approach to Smiggin Holes I thought the scenery was stunning; but I was becoming increasingly worried that I could see a hobbitish shape following us.
After the previous troubles on our Ozyssey,
I wondered what it could be.
Elle was walking beside me, and I asked if she'd seen something. She confirmed my suspicions, saying she'd seen movement parallel to us for some time.
We entered a forest half an hour later, and I feared the shape was closing in on us. Then I felt something snatch at my head, and before I knew it, I was hatless. My emerald cork hat had been pinched from right in front of my eyes; or right above my eyes to be precise.
I was bewildered by the bonce burglary, but Elle must have seen it coming; she was after the viperous varmint before I regained my composure.
The others joined me, and we set off after them, catching up on the third ridge.
Elle was holding the hobbitish creature by the scruff of the neck. Meanwhile, it was holding the emerald cork hat close to its chest, while repeating the sentence, 'my precious, my precious, it's mine, it's mine, it's Smiggin's hat, all mine...'

Notes

Lord of the Rings featured a hobbit called Sméagol / Gollum, who acted in a similar way to Smiggin, only it was a ring that was its 'precious'.

Zemanta's 'green' images of snake and various objects inspired the direction in the next two blogs.

----

97. SMIGGIN HOLES, HOLICULTURIST

I asked Smiggin for my hat back. It started handing it to me, and we both had a hold of it; but then it tried to grab it back, saying, 'no, no, it's mines, mines, it's Smiggin's hat.'

Magic of the Emerald Cork Hat

I tugged at the hat, but couldn't break it free from Smiggin's grip. While we grappled, heaps of other green objects fell from its person; I don't know where they all came from.
I lost concentration, and Smiggin must have seen its chance, because it pulled at the hat with much more strength than anything previously. It freed the hat from my grip, and I fell back, landing in a grave-size hole that had just appeared behind me.
Angry helped me out of the hole. Elle was still holding Smiggin, using her body fantastically well.
I looked at Smiggin, it smirked back.

The Case of Smiggin Holes is Solved

I asked Smiggin if it had anything to do with the hole. It continued smirking.
Angry approached me, and suggested that the ability to create holes would explain the second half of Maisie's Smiggin Holes warning.
It all made sense now. I congratulated Angry on an impressive use of his mind.

98. HAT-TRICK TO HOLE IN SMIGGIN HOLES

I could see no way of regaining my hat, and mentioned this to Cathy. She said that's not the spirit, before seeming to enter into a deep trance.

Snake Scares Smiggin Senseless

I couldn't believe my eyes a minute later, but luckily Smiggin did. The hat suddenly seemed to turn into a snake, and Smiggin quickly threw it into the air.
It flew a few feet, opening up into a full ten-foot length, before coiling back and once again becoming the emerald cork hat I'd grown to know and love. I dived to regain it, catching it one-handed two-feet off the three-dimensional floor.

Smiggin Creates Another Hole

I was looking forward to a soft landing in a mush of muddy earth and crisp leaves, when the ground opened up below me. I heard a cackle from Smiggin, and guessed it'd used its potent powers to open up another hole below where I was about to land.
The holiculturist had done itself proud with this one; it was more mineshaft than grave. I faced falling into a hole from which I didn't know if I'd ever be able to emerge.

99. SNAKES AND LADDERLESS HOLES FOR SNAGGIN' SMIGGIN

I mentally prepared myself for a long fall into a deep chasm, but then the hole suddenly moved to the left, and I landed head-first in a muddy puddle. I didn't even have my hat on to cushion the fall; but was relieved I'd avoided the hole.

Smiggin Holes is Down in a Hole

After I'd sat up and wiped the mud from my eyes, I saw the hole had moved under where Smiggin had been. Elle was standing beside the hole, but the holiculturist was nowhere to be seen.
I put my hat back on, and it felt good to be reunited with ol' corky. We all gathered around the hole. Smiggin was sitting at the bottom of it; looking disconsolate but still clutching some of its green hoard.

Cathy Keeps Quiet about Snaggin' Smiggin

I asked Cathy how she'd turned the hat into a snake and moved the hole. She said we all have our own special powers, and they wouldn't be special if everybody knew about them. Being a shapeshifting, chameleonic one-half of a legendary vegetarian werewolf I just had to agree with her, and left it at that.

Notes

Snakes and ladders is a popular board game.
Down in a Hole is an Alice in Chains song.

----

100. AUSTRALIA'S GREYTEST TRAVELLERS REACH THE CAPITAL

We left Smiggin Holes where it was, and headed east on the dust sandy path. I thought we'd left the *Lord of the Rings* influence behind, but that turned out to be nonsense, because I was reminded of it again when we stopped for supper: a berry dal in Berridale.

Can Berryer in Canberra

We were berry impressed with the berries in the dal, and it made us all feel much berrter after our Smiggin Holes ordeal. So we thought we'd try to go beyond the pain berryer; searching for more berries even if it meant a long endurance journey. Angry suggested trying Canberra, as he thought we could berryer there. And you know what, he was right, you can berryer in Canberra. It didn't take long before we were berrying an incrediberryble amount of berries into our bellies. I don't know what type the Canberra berries were; maybe cranberries with the r left out.

Missing Dairymans Plains Makes My Mind Complains

We headed back down south once our berry ballooned bellies felt balanced, but we made slow progress; because we took along some sloe berries. However, the sloe berries did satisfy my desire for more berries and set my mind at rest; because prior to berrying them, I'd been regretting our decision not to detour to Dairymans Plains, as it sounded good for a raspberry ripple.
It was getting late as we approached Cooma.

Notes

Dale is a region and battle in *Lord of the Rings*.
Dal is an Indian food pulse dish.

Berry language: berry – very, berrter – better, pain berryer – pain barrier, can berryer - Canberra, berrying – burying, incrediberryable - incredible.

----

101. COO MA, IT'S THE PIGEON MOTHERS OF COOMA

We didn't know what Cooma could provide at the late hour we arrived. Our bellies were all berried out, and seemed to have been racing to rumble the roarest more than our legs had been spinning to speed the slickest. My hopes rose at the Cooma city limits when we were met by a pigeon in a pinafore that was quick to come to the fore.

Pigeon Mothers of Cooma

She cooed a welcoome and introduced herself as Patricia. She said she was one of the many pigeon mothers of Cooma, although she'd been named after her grandmother, who was a member of *The Partridge Family*.
Patricia said they'd heard we were on our way from the pigeons in Coorow; the Coorowgeons had sent a carrier with a message about our journey. As time passed, they'd thought it must be literary nonsense, and Coorow had just wanted something to coo about; but our arrival meant it had not been nonsense after all. It had all turned out cooshty in the end.

Notes

The not nonsense phrase was probably inspired by Joseph Heller's *Catch-22*, which the author was reading at the time.
cooshty – cushty is slang for good.
The Partridge Family was a television series.

----

102. GOODBYE COO PIGEONS, HELLO BANJO BADGERS

The Coomageons put on a fine feast for us. We thanked them with full contented stomachs that rumbled no more. They sensed our satisfaction, and said it was the least they could do, after I'd shown the Coorowgeons the utmost respect. We offered to do the dishes, but they would hear none of it. Patricia was eager to show us their library, which was open twenty-four hours a day. The Coomageons were very proud of the renowned local poet, Samuel Cooleridgeon, and one room was devoted entirely to his works. One of his most notable poems was called *The Coomplaint of Ninathoma*.

Tara to Cooma

At the end of the night, we were escorted to lofts they'd converted for us. They had done a grand job, and I couldn't remember sleeping anywhere as coosy and coomfortable. In the morning, they coooked us up a coolity local delicacy they call pigidge. It was oat so delicious. As we tucked in, I told Patricia how impressed I was with the loft. Her response was most humble; she said they had been working on them for many moons.
Yes, I suppose they had had a lot of time.
My mind split into two halves. One imagined the pigeons working on the lofts, and the other remembered notable events from our Ozyssey; times when I had never heard of Cooma, didn't know where we were going, or if we'd survive. Angry noticed I wasn't eating and asked if I was alright. I thought it was a very perceptive use of his mind. I said, 'Yes, Angry, never been better... as one half of the Greenygrey anyway.' Angry laughed, and the others joined in.
Patricia said I had a 'good sense of coomour.' I laughed, and said she did too.
It was then time to say goodbye, and we left Cooma with a heavy heart and stomach. We could hear them cooing their farewells until we entered the Badja State Forest, and the chattering of badgers took over.

It was nice to walk through the thick forest at first, but then we reached a swamp, and it looked like it could get tricky. The dust sandy path was hardly visible at times, and we struggled to make much progress. I was contemplating asking the others if they could think of a quicker way through, when Angry said he could hear a banjo in the distance.

I thought he'd turned more crazy than angry for a minute, but it wasn't long before we could all hear it. We followed the direction of the sound, and emerged into a clearing where we could see a badger picking at a banjo. Angry pulled out his bagpipes and started playing along, and they were soon raising the canopy with their badger blues beats.

Notes

Tara – slang for goodbye.
Obscure pigeon words: coolity – quality. coomour – humour.
Samuel Coleridge (1772-1834) was a Romantic writer and poet. *The Complaint of Ninathoma* was one of his poems.
----

103. EAST COAST VIEW SUGGESTS JOURNEY'S END LOOMS?

Once they'd finished their banjo-bagpipes duel, Angry greeted the badger and complimented it on its playing, before introducing us all. The badger said its name was Badge, and called its parents out from their sett. Badge introduced them as Brock and Brocc.

Staying Dry in Dampier

Brock said they'd been expecting us, after the badgers of the Badginarra National Park told them we were on our way. I thought that was a coincidence, after we'd just benefited from a similar west-east communication between the pigeons of Coorow and Cooma.
The Badja badgers quickly arranged a clan meal, and the fine spread filled us up after the long hike. When we told them of our difficulty during the day they offered us a badger barge they had, and said it would deliver us through the forest.
We were overjoyed at this, and Angry gave them his bagpipes in return. Bakers' dozens of badgers emerged to see us off, badgering and barging one another to be on the best balcony.

Barging Through Dampier

We had a wonderful time barging through Dampier. It was thankfully nothing like the experience those poor people had in the film *Deliverance*, which I'd half suspected we might suffer after the duelling instruments reminded me of the film.
The river returned us to the dust sandy path, and a long uphill trek.

From a treetop
in a rest stop
outside Nerrigundah,
Elle had a gander,
her observation she did ponder

if it was the east coast yonder.
I was inspired by the tree scenery
to write this observation poetry;
was it the beginning of the end
the east to north Ozyssey bend.

We all rushed up the tree for a gander, and were happy to unanimously confirm Elle's discovery. I could see the east coast; all this time after starting off in the south-west. Nostalgia and optimism coursed through my veins, fused in my heart, and surged upwards to mind.

104. POTATOES AND CHEESE MAKE TRAVELLING A BREEZE

I slept well, and everybody else said they did too. There seemed a new energy in the camp, and we had a good start to our day's ramble; reaching Eurobodalla by mid-morning, and Bodalla around midday. They were quite similar towns, but Eurobodalla reminded me more of Europe for some reason.

We were going to stop in Bodalla for lunch, but then read about the South Coast Cheese just outside town, so went there instead. We picked up some right cheesy bargains at the factory shop; and I don't mean of the inauthentic kind. We couldn't wait to reach Potato Point after that, and had no trouble finding it. We just followed the pointing potatoes.

Reaching the East Coast at Potato Point

The Tasman Sea expanded with each step as we approached the east coast, and washed over us like a giant wet towel after we all jumped in upon arrival.

I had finally reached the east coast of Oz after arriving near the west coast over a year ago. I thought of Bonzo, and how he would no doubt have loved the refreshing relief of the neverending waves. But he was in a happy place. Upon emerging from the sea, and drying off, we set about cooking our dinner.

After an hour or three,
we had a tea fit for King Eddie,
and Queen Eloise,
of potatoes and cheese.

Notes

King Edward is a type of potato.

----

105. BUNGEE JUMPERS OF BINGIE SPLASH AND BRASH

I awoke on the beach. The sun shining through white cloud looked like a fried egg. I thought it'd go well with all our potatoes. Then,
there seemed to be a commotion in the Tasman Sea,
I wondered what it could be.

Brainwaves by the Waves

I slept again, before being awoken by a regular splashing in our locality. I thought somebody might have left a tap on, but then remembered we were on a beach and I had seen no taps nearby.
I was dozing back to sleep when a disturbing thought suddenly entered my noggin: all the early morning activity could be the MoMo East returning from the deep after its epic battle with MiMo Moby; or Smiggin escaped from its hole. I bolted upright, on the crest of a brainwave.
I was relieved to see it was not MoMo, oh no; or Smiggin, thank holiculturing; but some bungee jumpers that seemed to be arriving from a great distance.

Bingie Bungees Buzzing

Adopting a posh phone voice I once heard spoken in an old film, I said, 'Hey, hold on old chaps, don't you think it is jolly early for that kind of caper?'
I realised the one who answered must be a local when it buzzed, 'Strewth cobber, it's never too early for some bonzer fun like this.'
I just had time to ask where they were bungeeing from before they started the reverse journey. I thought I heard one buzz they were bungeeing from Bingie before they bounced out of sight.

106. BUNGEE TO BINGIE BEGUN BY A BEE

The others stirred soon after, and Angry asked about all the noise. I explained about the bungees from Bingie. I was worried Angry may get angry, but he remained calm. After seeming lost in thought for a minute, he suggested we ask the bungeeists if we could hitch a lift north. I thought it was a great use of his mind.

Can You Ride Tandem?

When the next bungeeists appeared from the north, Angry asked if we could hitch a lift to Bingie. One buzzed it would be no problem, and that they'd arrange for four tandem bungees to be used next time.
We packed up our gear, including a few spare spuds, and waited for our lifts. It was not long before four bungees appeared over the horizon.
It was a bit of a mad scramble, but we all got onto a bungee, and were soon flying through the air on our way to Bingie. It was only after I was on the bungee that I realised the pilot was a bee. And he was a very happy bee indeed. His obvious love for bungeeing was infectious, and I couldn't wait to get bungeeing. It didn't disappoint.
It was a truly exhilarating ride, and ended too quickly for my liking. We all landed beerilliantly in Bingie, and were as happy as Larry Bee. That was the name of my pilot.

Notes

'Can you ride tandem?' was a phrase used in a PG Tips advert starring bicycle-riding chimps in 1971.
Happy as Larry is an idiom meaning very happy; it is thought to have originated in Australia or New Zealand.

----

107. BINGIE BUNGEE BEES AND KALBARRI BARRY

We thanked the bees for the bungee to Bingie, and were about to leave, but then one flew over to us. She introduced herself as Beeatrice, before asking us not to buzz off straightaway, as they were having a beebeecue on the beeach that night.

A beebee on Bingie beach with Beeatrice and the bungeeing bees was too much to resist, so we quickly agreed in unison. We spent the afternoon chilling in the sea, and evening soon came.

Barry Joins Bee BBQ

We'd filled our bellies and were enjoying a tinny
or two with beeautiful company
when I thought I heard a familiar click out at sea
and then realised it was Kalbarri Barry.

After calling him over, I asked what he was doing all the way over the other side of Oz. He said he was holidaying with the family. I thought it was an amazing coincidence that we were both in Bingie at the same time, but you know, these things happen on the road... and at sea.

Barry Suggests Sydney

Barry said they were setting off for Sydney the next day, and invited us along. I hadn't shapeshifted for a while, so I suggested I shift into a bottlenose and swim with Barry and his family; pulling the others behind us on a makeshift raft. Everybody agreed to the idea, and we constructed the raft after the beerilliant bbq finished.

As the last embers of the fire lost their glow, we fitted the harness to the raft using the moonlight that silverlined across the ocean to our place on the sand.

108. BYE-BYE BINGIE, WE'RE OFF ON A BOTTLENOSE FANTASY

I slept well, and the others all seemed ready to leave when I first looked up. They were chatting jollily, and there seemed to be another new spirit amongst them.

Buzzing Off from the Bees of Bingie

The bees provided a beeautiful brekkie of honey beescuits. I felt a new surge of energy flow through my body afterwards.

After brekkying
on beescuits
we packed away
and made our way
out to sea
for parley
with Barry
and family.

Be Safe said the Bees All at Sea

The bees flew out as far as the first horizon, which was the limit of their safe flight range; but some bungeed a little farther. They all sang goodbyee. It was a beeautiful sight from the early morning ocean, lit up aquamarine by the new day's sun.
The harness and raft worked well. Barry and I swam in the front, with Barry's wife and three calves in two rows behind us.

It felt dynamite to be a dolphin again yessiree,
freely swimming in the wild open sea,
bounding as a bottlenose with great company,
although it was a shame to leave the bees of Bingie.

109. MOLLY MOOK'S ROWDY ROOK IN ULLADULLA

We made good progress through the clear morning, and it didn't seem long before Ulladulla came into view.

Barry beaked my attention
toward an approaching bird,
we slowed down as it neared.
When the bird arrived overhead,
it stretched out its wings and said:

'Ahoy, sailors and swimmers,
you look in need of dinners.
I am Molly Mook,
landlady of the Rowdy Rook,
and I invite you to our snug nook.'

I said we were doing well,
but the offer sounded as swell
as the wave just approaching,
so how faraway is the Rook
as the crow flies, Molly Mook.

Molly laughed, before saying, 'It is nine nautical miles as the crow flies, and I should know, for I am one; not a rook, I am a crow, and I fly as the crow flies.'
It didn't sound a vast detour, and Molly seemed a chirpy character, so with the consent of the others I agreed:

'We'd like to visit the Rowdy Rook,
so without a second look,
please lead us there chuck.'

The Rowdy Rook has a Familiar Look

Molly said the harbour would be busy, so she led us to the beach above. From there, we walked down Ocean Street to the Rowdy Rook; I'd shapeshifted out of dolphin by then of course!

The Rowdy Rook was as welcoming as Molly had suggested. It was full of corvids of all types, and played some vids that made you think cor! The Black Crowes, Byrds and Them Crooked Vultures were particularly amazing.

We were ravenous by the time our mag pies arrived, and they fitted the bill; stylishly served in plates shaped like a spoonbill bill. That was some cook at the Rook.

Notes

Ocean Street and Mollymook are in Ulladulla
Corvids are groups of birds of the corvidae biological family; such as crows, ravens, jays and magpies.
Black Crowes, Byrds and Them Crooked Vultures are all real bands.

---

110. ROWDY ROOK PUSHES BODY, MIND AND SPIRIT TO LIMIT

The chirpy atmosphere continued into the afternoon. Elle was playing darts with a kingfisher called Kingsley; Cathy was dancing flamenco with a flamingo, and Angry was playing chess with a rook.

Stepping on Toe, Flamingo

Several dances later, the flamingo was visibly starting to tire, and stepping on Cathy's feet; but Cathy kept dancing until the end of the song, which showed steadfast spirit. Then she seemed to make her excuses before returning to our table.

Cathy asked if it was time to flit
as it seemed to be getting late
long time since leaving Barry
and his fantastic family.
I looked at the timekeeping cuckoo,
and was shocked to clock
how many times it had gone tick-tock.
Time flies when you're having fun
with birds, there are no hands to turn.

Rounding up the Team

I agreed it was probably time to go, and we went over to tell Elle first. I asked her if she was ready to leave, but she replied, 'Hold on cobber, I just need a bullfinch's eye to win this deciding game.' Then she threw it straight in the middle, looking confident in her body. Kingsley was a little crestfallen, but gallant in defeat.
I moseyed over to see how Angry was getting on. He'd just cornered the rook's king with his rook and king, which I thought showed great mental dexterity. The rook was very sporting, although it had a disappointed look.

Leaving the Rowdy Rook

I shouted to Molly Mook that we had to leave the Rowdy
Rook, and thanked her for the hospitality. She thanked us for
our custom. The others gave us the bird; in a nice way.
We returned to the beach, singing and swaying as we went.
Seeing our bottlenose buddies still swimming in the serene
sea capped off a delightful day.

Notes

clock - slang for look.

---

111. SKY SHOW LEADS TO SWAN LAKE STORY

As we prepared to set off
I thought I heard a commotion
out in the Tasman Sea,
and wondered what it might be.
However, when I looked around, the ocean was calm. None
of the others seemed to have noticed anything, so I kept it to
myself.

Green Ray and Epic Ballet

The moon had risen by the time we reached the Bendalong
peninsula, and its light was invaluable as we bent our route
around Bendalong for a long time.
It was dawn by the time we reached Swan Lake via
Cudmirrah. The sunrise's crepuscular rays streaked up into
the bluing sky.
The lake's name reminded me of the ballet; from what I
remembered, it was a tale every bit as epic as this one.
I thought I saw a green ray above the sun as it rose; I
wondered if it was a sign from Green, or the rare optical
phenomenon I'd read about.
Those last two thoughts seemed to trigger my next one: that
it would be more like Green to compare its journey to
something so grandeur as *Swan Lake*.
After so much thinking early in the morning I half wished I
was back in human form instead of being a brainwaving
bottlenose; so I could neck a few Swan beers!

Notes

The Swan brewery is in Perth.

I shapeshifted into human form after we moored on the edge of *Swan Lake*, and looked up the *Swan Lake* tale on Wikipedia before going to Cudmirrah with the people. Barry and family were happy to lounge in the lake.

Swan Lake Cudmirrah *Swan Lake*

A man approached us on the edge of town and introduced himself as Prince Siegfried. I said I was pleased to meet him, but thought twice about that after his next words.
He said he was about to harpoon me when I was a dolphin; but then he saw me change into a human, and fell madly in love with me.
I thought this Cudmirrah Swan Lake situation could mirror the *Swan Lake* plot a little too much for my liking.
So I said I was just passing through, and although very flattered, wouldn't be able to spend any time with him. He looked a tad disappointed, but seemed to accept it.
We continued into Cudmirrah, which is a lovely town in a beautiful setting, and stocked up on provisions for the onward journey.
We were about to leave the lake and head out to open sea, when we saw the prince dive into the far end of the lake. An older woman shouted, 'Siegfried, no, don't do it, come back.'

Swan Lake Tragedy

I was shocked, but didn't want to get involved. Barry said he wanted to help, so he untied his harness, and started swimming toward the prince; his wife and children followed, hot on his tailfluke.
We watched them closely, and paid a heavy price for it. For as our dolphin friends rose out of the water and into the air, half-way there, a salvo of harpoons landed all amongst and around them.
I finally broke free of my harness, and set off to look for our bottlenose buddies, but half-way there I saw them ascending

into the ether; clicking and smiling with what looked like love, just the same as when they'd played in the water. It was a scene straight out of Swan Lake, literally and metaphorically.

Notes

In Tchaikovsky's *Swan Lake* (1875-1876), Prince Siegfried falls in love with Odette, who is turned into a swan by sorcery. It was inspired by Russian folk tales.

----

113. SWAN LAKE MUST BE A TRAGEDY, KNEW BARRY

I returned to the others with a heavy heart, hardly believing what I had just witnessed: The ocean losing the life and beauty of Barry and his bottlenose family just like that.

Losing Friends is a Tragedy

I remembered our first contact in Kalbarri, all those moons ago, and over the other side of the continent; how Barry had saved Bonzo and me from a storm, while sending us to Meekatharra for our first meeting with MiMo Moby.
I ploughed through an ocean that suddenly seemed against me; gently lapping waves now felt arrow-sharp. It was in complete contrast to the morning, when the same sea had seemed to lift me through the waves with energy, love and vibrancy; but to what it must not have known.
Maybe it now shared my mourning, or punished me as I chastised myself. I felt somehow responsible. If I hadn't contacted Barry in Kalbarri, and seen him in Bingie, maybe he and his family would still be making their way up the east coast.
I'd also been thinking grand thoughts more suited to Green than myself; had I overstepped my boundaries?

Body, Mind and Spirit Rescue the Situation

My trepidation increased as I approached the others, still not knowing how I would tell them the terrible news. As I approached the raft, Cathy jumped in the ocean and swam to me.
I was about to tell her the news, when she said it was okay, they already knew Barry and family had left us; she had also seen them rising into the ether. I was thankful to Cathy for raising my spirits a little as I climbed up to join the others.
Angry provided further comfort when he said Barry had recited a farewell note to him as we approached Cudmirrah. He gave me the note:

In his letter to me,
Barry said it was meant to be,
Swan Lake must be a tragedy,
I have accepted the inevitability,
of the dolphin tale calamity.
I want you to feel better,
so I wrote you this letter.

I was touched by Barry's sentiment, and relieved that he was
prepared for what happened. I was also thankful to Angry for
a thoughtful use of his mind.
I asked the others what we should do now, without Barry and
family to pull the raft. Elle said she was feeling strong, and
would join me in the harness. I thought it would be an
incredibly helpful use of her body, and quickly thanked her.
Having decided our futures, we rested for a few hours and
mourned our lost friends; softly singing salutations to the
smiling cetaceans.

114. HUSKY SON IN HUSKISSON HUSHES US ON

Elle took to the raft-pulling like a dolphin to water, and with a lighter load on a calmed sea we reached similar speeds to the previous day. It felt refreshing to be back amongst the waves, alternating between waterworld and skyspace, although I was still missing Barry and family of course.

Huskisson has Potent Pull

We reached Jervis Bay in the evening, and thought about stopping somewhere for a meal.
As we circled the bay from the left, Vincentia didn't draw us in, but Huskisson seemed to have a certain pull.

Mooning in Moona Moona

We were preparing to land near Elizabeth Drive, on the junction with Moona Moona Creek, when a car full of women stopped at a nearby junction.
The driver mooned at us twice. Her front-seat passenger berated her, 'Elizabeth, will you stop mooning or we'll be up the Creek without a paddle; there's a husky father and son just over there. Elizabeth, drive on now.'
The husky son just chuckled, and hushed us on.

115. WALL ON GONG IN WOLLONGONG KEEPS US MOVING ON

We continued travelling north up the east coast, thinking we'd overnight in Wollongong. We stopped in Shell Cove to re-energise, and were served by a friendly snail called Michelle.

Her shell reminded me of lobsters, and I told her I hadn't seen any around. 'chelle replied with the cove-shaped *Ode of Shell Cove*:

There were 110 lobsters eating pears
contentedly up a crab-apple tree.
When along came a storm
and swept them out to sea.
They made themselves at home
and decided that's where they'd be.

I thanked her for letting me know, and providing the energy, before bidding farewell.

War gorillas, War is wrong and Wall on gong

As we passed Warilla we saw gorillas warring on the beach. I was amazed to see this, as the gentle giants are usually very peaceful.

This was confirmed when we reached Warrawong, because the beach was full of gorillas holding a peace protest proclaiming 'War is wrong'.

Strange events relating to place names seemed to be the theme of the day, because approaching Wollongong we heard a deafening gong sound from that direction. I wondered if we should land at Wollongong, as planned. The decision was made for us when we approached the city, because there was a massive wall all around it, just above the gong.

So we continued past, hearing the gonging grow louder off Wollongong, and reach its decibel zenith parallel with

Battery Park. Somewhere between Wombarra and Scarborough we sensed the sounds of silence again.

Notes

Simon and Garfunkel covered *Scarborough Fair*, an old British ballad. They also had a song and album called *Sounds of Silence*.

----

116. ARRIVING IN SYDNEY, BOOKED BY BRONTE

Moon moves milky
waves washing whales
rising rolling roaming
entrancing ethereal eternal.

Sighting Sydney is a Sight for Salty Eyes

Sea and shore were serenely silent for seventeen hours on
the approach to Sydney. Just before reaching land
I thought I saw a commotion
farther out in the Tasman Sea,
and wondered what it could be.
However, the sea was calm moments later. None of the
others seemed to have seen it, so I didn't say anything. There
wasn't time anyway, as we had to decide where to dock.

Docking at Sydney

Cronulla looked made of vanilla
Coogee appeared too easy
so we landed at Bronte
as it seemed to have something to say.
There was no time for wuthering
as the winds reached record heights.
We saw a woman by the name of Jane Eyre
fly head over heels all up in the air
dropping a book our way
by the name of Agnes Grey.

Notes

Brontes and books (*Wuthering Heights* by Emily Bronte,
Agnes Grey by Anne Bronte, Jane Eyre by Charlotte Bronte).
----

117. INTO THE LAIR OF THE PADDINGTON BEAR

I wondered if a book of Grey was a sign, and quickly flicked
through it. Although it was certainly not literary nonsense, it
did not seem to have much relevance to my life or journey.
So I didn't investigate further, and donated it to the Bronte
library Bronte section.

Whatever will be, will be,
and if Agnes Grey re-enters my story,
I will return to the Bronte area library,
and look it up under section Bronte.

Paddington Bear Gives us a Scare

We walked up through Bondi at quite a pace,
and were resting five minutes in Paddington place,
when a colourful bear entered the street
marching purposely in wellington-booted feet.

He looked harmless, dressed in an old coat and hat, and
carrying a big suitcase, but you never know! He came right
up to us and asked if this was the right direction for Peru.
Funnily enough, I'd seen a boat departing to Peru in a day or
two on Bondi Beach, so I told the Paddington Bear.
He thanked me, and gave us a marmalade sandwich each
before saying adios.

Notes

Paddington Bear (Michael Bond creation).

----

118. SPIT THE DOG RESERVED IN SYDNEY

We continued north to the Opera House, where I felt like a proper tourist, and not a bedraggled traveller from another dimension. We looked at a Sydney map there, and one place stood out straight away: the Spit Reserve. I was a big fan of Spit the Dog when it starred on *Tiswas*, and thought the reserve must be where it now resided.

Crossing the Harbour Bridge to the Spit Reserve

The others agreed to go there, so we made our way across Harbour Bridge to the north, with great views of Little Sirius Cove below. Pebbles glinted in the sunshine like stars on a clear night. Mosman reminded me of that Mothman creature I met while one half of the Greenygrey on our epic ramble across North America. Magical memories momentarily materialised once more.

There was a Spit Road leading to the Spit Reserve. I was impressed with the amount of respect they had bestowed upon my favourite puppet dog.

Entering the Spit Reserve was like every Spit the Dog fan's dream, as there were dozens of the dogs all enjoying life in safety; although I couldn't be sure if I saw the original Spit amongst them.

They seemed reserved compared to the original Spit, with not much wild spitting going on at all; I guess the passing of time in such a comfortable reserve had mellowed the spitline out.

Notes

Spit the Dog was a puppet worked by Bob Carolgees on *Tiswas* (1970s/1980s fun variety show).

----

119. DR. WATSON AND THE CASE OF A GREYCLIFFE HOUSE MOUSE

The Spit Reserve was so relaxing we didn't want to leave, and they had to spit us out at closing time. We wondered where to go next. Not liking the sound of Hunters Bay, we thought about the Sydney Harbour National Park. The headquarters and visitor centre was called Greycliffe House, which I thought was worth investigating. So we walked that way.

Dr. Watson of Watsons Bay

Upon arrival at Greycliffe House, I was surprised to find it was neither particularly grey nor built on a cliff. As we looked around, a gentleman introduced himself as a guide, and said his name was Dr. Watson. I asked him why the house was called Greycliffe. He apologised for not knowing, explaining that he was only an expert on nearby Watsons Bay. The expert on Greycliffe House, a chap called Holmes, was away researching some other homes at the moment.

The Greycliffe House Mouse

Not long after I'd thanked Dr. Watson and turned away,
in a triangular hall containing a square ball,
I was accosted by a small mouse of my colour grey.

It said its name was Cliff and the house was named after him,
I replied it was built in 1852 so how could that be true,
It said it was on a special diet and low-fat cheese kept it quiet.

I thought, *Now, that's nonsense.*

Notes

Walk This Way – Aerosmith song, later shared with Run DMC.

The author had been reading about Edward Lear's literary nonsense poems just before writing this, and the poem is perhaps the closest to Lear's style in this book.
Sherlock Holmes and Dr. Watson (Arthur Conan Doyle's famous fictional detectives).

---

120. THE BARANGAROO KANGAROO IS JUST A SHORT HOP OR TWO

It was getting late,
and I didn't wanna wait,
but the others were deep,
in conversation of sleep,
so I had forty winks,
and fourteen thinks.
I was awoken by the others,
who said a lady named Carruthers,
and her four brothers,
were heading to Bronte's Wuthers,
and we could go along,
if we didn't take too long.

Travelling Sydney by Ferry Taxi

So I jumped up, leaving twelve intellectual thoughts behind,
and taking two nonsense ones along. We ran to the beach,
and a ferry taxi soon picked us up.

The captain was a kangaroo
who said it lived in Barangaroo;
down on Darling Harbour,
south of Goat Island's ardour;
above Sydney aquarium's
somewhat fishy delirium.
Life was usually fun in town
apart from the Rolf
trying to tie it down.

I thought, *That Rolf again.* I said it must be nice living just a
short hop or two from so many interesting places.

121. BONGIN BONGIN BAY AFTER CURL CURL CURL DEE WHY

We thanked Captain 'roo from 'roo for a pleasant passage back to Bronte, and said farewell to the Carruthers siblings when they headed inland. Our raft was still there, so it was back on the ocean waves for us.

Dee Why? Curl Curl Curl

Elle and I put our harnesses on, and were about to set off,
when I looked behind me
and thought I could see
a commotion in the Tasman sea.
I wondered what it could be.
I glanced at the others, but nobody seemed to have seen it;
and when I looked back out to sea there was nothing to see.
So we set off north, curling far and wide around Curl Curl.
Our curl was obviously quite a spectacular one, as it was
noticed faraway. How do I know that? Because when we
reached Dee Why, a deer called Dee asked why we'd curled
around Curl Curl. I said it was a natural curl.

Bongin Bongin Bay is a Nice Place to Stay

We reached Bongin Bongin Bay by midnight, after Cathy had guided our way by the moonlight silverline.

Silverlining sea
lunar symmetry
sunlight rhapsody
projecting harmony.

Once settled on the beach, we started a fire with washed up
dry wood, and talked while eating before falling asleep under
a starry sky.
I dreamt of a commotion out at sea
and wondered what it might be.

122. SIRENS SOUND SWEET TO ME, BUT NOT CATHY

We awoke on the sand
between sea and land
of the rising sun
I have much to learn.

We ate the leftovers from the previous night before setting off. They helped us make good progress, despite a swirling wind picking up off Mona Vale port, sounding like Vale Park when the Valiants are losing.
At the end of the morning we passed Dolphin Bay, and I thought of Barry and family. I wished they were still with us to see the bay full of delightful dolphins.
I was cheered somewhat by Cheero Point, and a little more by Little Wobby.

The Tug Under the Norah Jones Siren

The going got tough parallel to Tuggerah Lake, as the current tugged us toward the coast as if trying to tie us together. I was beginning to weaken when Elle took up most of the strain, which I thought was an impressive use of her body. I'd just recovered from that when I heard some beautiful music lilting over to us from Norah Head. The songs seemed to be saying sweet nothings like: '*Love Me Tender*', '*Thinking About You*', '*Come Away With Me*' and '*Until The End*'.
I started swimming toward Norah Head, and Elle followed my lead. The next thing I remember, Cathy was putting ear-plugs in my ears, and then doing the same to Elle. We stopped swimming and looked up; and saw we were seconds away from crashing into the rocks. I asked Cathy what had drawn us toward the Norah Head coast, and she replied *Siren*. It was a narrow escape for us, and I was extremely grateful that Cathy had been on the same spirit level.

Notes

The Valiants playing at Vale Park are Port Vale, an English football league team.

Norah Jones and songs: *Love Me Tender, Thinking About You, Come Away With Me* and *Until The End.*

The Sirens' songs summoned sailors onto rocks in Greek mythology.

---

123. CORRIE SOAP BEFORE BOOMERANG DASHES GREEN HOPE

Being in the sea didn't mean we missed out on seeing land animals. Why, while passing Wommara Avenue we saw a wombat hitch-hiking to the Masai Mara; and on Kalaroo Road we saw a kangaroo either side of LA.

We stopped for a wash at the Corrie Island Nature Reserve, as it was overflowing with soap, and there were lots of spare brushes on the nearby Mungo Brush road.

We dried off under the whopper wind at the Wind Woppa Reserve.

Boomerang Wastes the Green Day

Feeling refreshed, we ate up the nautical miles at a good rate of knots in the afternoon, and a few hours later reached Boomerang Beach. That's when the day started going downhill; or to be more accurate, around and around.

Because once we stepped onto the beach we were thrown up into the air, and spun around at great speed over Elizabeth Beach and The Lakes Way.

I thought, *at least we're heading north, maybe it's a stroke of good fortune*. I saw Green Point ahead, and hoped it might be a sign: *maybe we'll land on a nice patch of green when we reach it.*

However, I hadn't taken the Boomerang part of the beach's name into consideration. The next moment, the return movement seemed to kick in over the Booti Booti National Park, and we just about reached Green Point before being spun south again.

We gathered pace on the southerly downhill, and before we had time to draw our breaths, we were descending to Boomerang Beach. I hoped the nightmare might end when we returned to the beach, but as soon as we neared the ground we were thrown back into the air for another circuit!

Notes

Corrie is a nickname for Coronation Street, a British soap opera.

----

124. SPIRIT LIFTS, MIND PLANS, BODY GIVES HOPE

I was getting sick of the sight of Boomerang Beach and Green Point by the twenty-ninth return journey, and told Cathy I was losing hope.

She said, 'That's not the spirit!'

That was the lift I needed; mentally I might add, as I certainly didn't need more physical lifting!

After Cathy raised my spirits, I wondered if Angry might have a solution to our situation, as he'd been using his mind well recently. So I asked him if he could think of any way out of our repetitive return rebounding.

He thought for a few minutes, before suggesting we'd been playing into the phantom boomerang's hands; or wings to be more precise.

Angry explained his rationale through the whistling wind: it was because the four of us had been keeping to a straight two-two formation, and this kept the boomerang on its preferred trajectory.

Come Elle or Eye Water

Angry suggested that Elle might be the key to changing our course, as she'd been using her body well recently. If we kept an eye on her, whether they were watery or not, and she pulled in one direction, we could all follow her, and that would hopefully release us from our eternal boomeranging. You know what, it didn't sound nonsense at all, and I had high hopes that it would finally ground us. We agreed to attempt it on our next northerly journey.

125. YAHOO FLIGHT TO THE LEFT AND RIGHT

I screamed, 'Thirtieth time lucky!' as we left Boomerang Beach and headed north over Elizabeth Beach once more.

We flew the Lakes Way,
knowing its outlay,
like night and day.

Yahoo! over Yahoo Island

It was all systems go, as Elle decided it was time to act, and we were primed to respond. She chose the Booti Booti National Park to kick the plan into action, leaning as much to the left as possible. We all followed her over to that side. We flew above and beyond Green Point, and seemed to have escaped the coastal cycle. We all exclaimed yahoo! over Yahoo Island. Green Point grew smaller every minute, and Boomerang Beach soon faded out of sight.

Wall in Gate Changes Our Plan

We were free-flying now, but just as we began to relax and enjoy the view, we saw a massive wall in a gigantic gate over Wallingat National Park. It would surely be the end of us if we crashed into it. Elle had seen the danger and jumped over to the right; we quickly followed. But was it too late?
We had stopped heading straight into the wall, and were now skirting it. Our chances of escape seemed finely balanced. We leant as much to the right as possible, while trying to push against the wall with our left arms. It was preventing our obliteration, but wasn't winning our liberation. That is, until our flying fate was decided twenty minutes later, once and for all.
A tower jutted out of the wall further on, blocking our side-skirting path. We flew closer and closer to it, and all my strength and spirit seemed nearly spent. I could see nothing beyond the tower, and no way of avoiding it. We were facing a dead-end in more ways than one.

Then Elle asked if we were ready, nodding toward the right. We all looked at her with renewed hope, not needing more explanation, and said yes. We prepared ourselves. Elle gave one almighty push, and we gave it our best too; it seemed to be working, as we were sent free of the wall. Then Elle leant to the right, and we followed her as the tower loomed; it was just enough, as we swerved around the tower into clear sky, with only a second or three to spare. It had probably been Elle's most outstanding use of her body yet.

Flying North-East, for a while at Least

We were flying in open air again, with no hazards in view. A north-easterly wind kept our direction and elevation steady. Maybe our luck was changing! We turned past Tuncurry in a hurry, and went even faster over Forster. I was beginning to enjoy the flight.
I should have known it wouldn't last. The wind dropped, and I got cramp in my rump;
I was like a dead-weight blowing in the breeze, dragging the team down to the trees.
We descended at pace, and the next thing I knew we were crashing into the Ocean Dreaming Rainforest Resort on the edge of Red Head.
When we'd recovered our composure I noticed the others had red heads after the bumpy landing. They said mine was still grey.

126. SWIMMING IN A WOAD SEA TO PORT MACQUARIE

Three red heads and a grey,
made their way,
to the bay.
Where the dust sandy road,
was lying overboard,
in a sea of woad.

Now raftless, we swam the dust sandy path, leading us north up the coast. It was good to be back on the ground, even if we were in the sea!
We were going to stop for a rest when we reached Crowdy Head, but a quick headcount suggested it was overcrowded.
So we continued swimming through afternoon into evening.

Pour Macawry in Port Macquarie

When the bright lights of Port Macquarie lit up the western horizon we decided to call it a day. It'd been quite some swim, no nonsense.
After drying off we popped into a beachside establishment called Two Cans Irish Pub. We walked up to the bar and a toucan asked us what we'd like to drink.
I knew toucans advertise Guinness, so we all asked for a pint of it. It started pouring one, while holding another pint in its other wing; and asked a macaw standing farther down the bar to pour the other two. The toucan and macaw had different styles of pouring, which could perhaps be called pour toucany and pour macawry.

Notes

Guinness is a stout beer.

----

127. EPIC POEM OF NSW NORTH COAST SEA JOURNEY

We had a good night in Macquarie,
slept well without hearing snory,
had a filling breakfast first thing,
and then it was time to get going.

Hat Head

We travelled slower than the day before,
as our arms ached and heads were sore,
Hat Head was therefore a welcome break,
and my emerald cork hat seemed to wake.

Coffs Harbour

We were ready for a drink by Nambucca Heads,
but quickly left when offered four sambuca reds,
Coffs Harbour looked nice but sounded dangerous,
for those vulnerable to colds and viral illness.

Korora

Then my hat seemed to be dragging me on,
as if to a faraway land in a time once upon,
we raced the Pacific Highway to Korora,
even though it meant missing an aurora.

Moonee Beach

Moonee Beach flashed right past,
with my hat changing gear to very fast,
I didn't know where we were going,
but the journey certainly wasn't boring.

Emerald Beach

Then I saw the beach ahead was green,

I think it was the limiest I'd ever seen,
so I thought I knew what my hat was up to,
and felt it could be this journey's breakthrough.

Notes

Sambuca is an alcoholic aniseed drink.
----

128. WELCOME TO THE JUNGLE: EMERALD FOREST BEACH

I grew ever more apprehensive as we neared Emerald Beach; because my last few experiences of green hadn't worked out well. There was our terrible episode with Smiggin Holes, Lord of the Green; the green ray I'd seen before our awful Swan Lake experience; and then we couldn't get past Green Point after being boomeranged from Boomerang Beach. I thought Green would probably have had much better luck at those places, and maybe I just wasn't cut out for this epic rambling lark.

Emerald Beach

My emerald cork hat almost dragged me onto Emerald Beach; it seemed to be growing in strength, and I now felt like it was wearing me more than the other way around! I took it off to have a look at it, and was shocked to find I could only see its corks. I put it back on and it pulled toward a crag jutting out of the cliff at the far side of the beach. I looked back at the others, who seemed to share my curiosity.
Moreover,
out of the corner of my eye,
in the seemingly faraway ocean,
I thought I saw a commotion,
and wondered what it could be.
It was difficult making our way through all the emerald; like struggling through dense jungle. But my hat was a good guide, and we soon reached the crag. I thought that might be it, but the hat wanted to go farther; it led me around the edge of the cliff. The others followed. I thought I knew what my hat was up to when we turned the corner. Emerald Beach had a secret cave.

Notes

The secret cave is inspired by adventure books such as those in Robert Arthur Jr's *The Three Investigators* series.

---

129. LIFE OF BRIAN'S BANE BELOW BRISBANE

My hat's excitement continued to grow; it seemed to be in the know.

We rushed into the cave, hurtling through the narrow passages as if time was of the essence. My hat seemed to be getting stronger with every step, and provided enough glow for us to see clearly; it felt like I was wearing a green neon sign pointing ahead.

I started singing 'Always look on the bright side of life...' and the others quickly joined in.

Brian the Baggy Green

We turned a corner, and I could see a colossal cavern complex ahead. It was full of people, animals... and other objects. My hat suddenly flew off and headed straight for a baggy green hat. They met in mid-air, and embraced passionately.

We looked in awe, as the green reunion shone like a golden wonder.

Life of Brian's Bane

When they returned to our level, my hat almost knocked me over without touching me, as it spoke for the first time.

It said, 'Hello Grey, my name is Emily, the Emerald Cork Hat. I'm sorry I couldn't talk to you before, but it would have been too dangerous for you. I had to wait until I was reunited with my other half, Brian the Baggy Green. It was foretold in historic hatlore that a greeny werewolf Halfling would survive a hat-trick of green tasks before reuniting the hats of hope here in the Emerald Beach cave. The union of green will lead to a top hat age of unpolluted peace and prosperity.'

I said, 'It's good to talk, and it's no problem about the previous lack of communication, but there is just one thing, for I am Grey.'

Emily seemed to smile, before asking me if I'd seen myself lately.

I looked down and was totally shocked to see that I was green all over. I had become green in the Emerald Cave without even realising it. It felt like a landmark moment, and I now felt confident I could achieve anything; just like I always think Green can. I felt like bouncing around the cave like a spring green.

However, Emily quickly brought me down to earth with a warning, 'There are still great tests ahead, and we will require your services again if you want to remain with us. We are heading north to our destiny; a war to end all wars. For Brian it is the bane of his life. If you join us, I'm sure we can win this one last great battle, and all return to the lives we desire.'

Notes

Baggy green hats have been worn by Australian cricketers for over a century. The author first heard of them on the sports quiz show, *Question of Sport*, just before reaching this stage of the book on the blog; over a year after starting to write it.
Life of Brian was a Monty Python film. It featured an Eric Idle song called 'Always Look on the Bright Side of Life.'
Golden Wonder is a crisp (American 'chips') making company.
Halfling is another name for a hobbit in *Lord of the Rings*.
'It's good to talk' was a strapline used in British Telecom adverts.

----

130. FOR THE LIFE OF BRIAN

I looked around at my travel companions, and they all nodded in unison. I had not doubted them. I told Emily we would be proud to join her in the battle of Bri's bane.
She thanked us, before inviting us to join the crowd in the cavern. She told me she thought I'd recognise a few faces.

Meeting Old Friends

There were indeed some familiar faces. I could hardly believe my eyes when they told my mind that Digger and Aussie, two of the first friends I made on the trip, were standing in front of me. It wasn't until I'd hugged them that I accepted it as bona fide. After catching up with my canine cohorts I introduced them to Angry, Cathy and Elle; because I hadn't even met them when I met ol' Dig and Aus. It all seemed such a long time ago now, and strange to think that I had landed in Oz all alone.
I was just getting over the surprise of Dig and Aus when there was a tap on my shoulder. When I looked around I saw yet another of my dear ol' friends from early in the journey: the very venerable Vombatus Ursinus. It was great to see it looking swell. Vombat the Wombat joined our circle and soon got to know everybody and everything.

Mine's a Large One

I was about half way through telling Vombat about my journey when the walls started to rumble, and some rocks broke off. Everybody looked at the epicentre with anticipation, while beginning to take guard. I wondered if it was a bulldozing blitz by Bri's bane.
A hole started to appear, and everybody tensed. As more rocks fell a paw emerged, and then the identity of the new arrivals was revealed. Why, it was none other than Colin and Ollie, the collie collier twins from Collie.

131. CHURCHILLA'S CHINCHILLA COMMANDOS OF GOYA

Reacquainting with the Collie twins was like digging into the past and striking pure gold; or maybe finding the best buns is a more appropriate metaphor when thinking about Bunbury's Collie twins. Everybody was enjoying the moment, although we knew that a bruising battle lay ahead with Bri's bane. We partied through the night, with a band of Beatles starring in the Cavern, and then headed north the next morning.

Liaising with the Chinchilla Chinchillas

Emily and Brian led us through the green-lit tunnels for ten hours, until we at last reached the safe haven of Chinchilla. The Chinchilla chinchillas were also locked in a perennial struggle with Bri's bane, so we were warmly welcomed. Emily and Brian introduced us all to the chinchilla leader, Pancho Churchilla, and he thanked us for our support. When evening arrived, we all ascended into the fresh air, and basked in the Chinchilla sunset chinchilla style.

Chinchillas of Goya

We rested overnight underground in the burrow barracks of the Chinchillas of Goya (COG); a crack unit of chinchilla commandos that are the teeth of the chinchilla army sprocket.
They gave us their nests and slept on the floor, as their training had hardened them to such inconvenience. I didn't like to take the nest, but we had been on a long hard journey; as long as the COG could maintain rotation without such self-maintenance.

Born to Bask

Someone had scrawled a message on the rock next to my nest that haunted my sleep that night. It said: Born to Bask, Live for Task.

It was signed CC, so I guess it must have been Cilla Chinchilla who wrote it; Pancho said she was the one who normally slept there. I thought it was a shame such a chilled chinchilla had to live this way, and dreamt that one day soon the chinchillas would be able to once more bask in peace.

We were awoken early. After a short preparation we started on our final march to Bri's bane. Nerves, excitement and fear all mixed together to activate anarchic adrenalin.

Notes

The Beatles found fame at the Cavern club.
Pancho Villa (Mexican revolutionary leader).
Winston Churchill (British Prime-Minister during World War Two).
Goya was a 19th century painter, and one of his paintings was named *Los Chinchillas*. The COG idea was set in motion when *Los Chinchillas* was suggested as an image on the *Werewolf of Oz* Wordpress blog by Zemanta.

----

132. THE CLIMB TO BRI'S BANE GREENSLOPES WITHOUT ROPES

Three hours after leaving Chinchilla we received word that a rock fall had blocked the tunnel. Colin and Ollie were informed, and soon raced ahead to clear the way. Their colliering skills meant we surfaced at The Gap gap on schedule. The sun was reaching its apex as the COG led us into the daylight of our destiny. I had faded to grey, and felt comfortable that way.

Emily and Brian led the COG commandos at the head of our line; I had never seen such courage from a pair of hats. Although they shone with a golden hue when first meeting again, nobody could accuse them of being yella in a cowardly way.

Talking of yellow, I was missing Emily not being on my head, with the scorching sun sizzling my sight and cooking my cranium! It was a relief when we reached some tree cover. We covertly met a covert of coots in the Mount Coot-Tha forest, and they escorted us easterly to rendezvous with a python called Pilly; it showed us a short-cut through a secret door at Indooroopilly.

Arriving at Greenslopes for the Battle of Bri's bane

Emerging through the outdoor, a river lay below us. Churchilla said it was Bri's bane's main defensive line. I couldn't imagine how all the furry little chinchillas were going to cross the river. I was in for another nice surprise. When we arrived at the river I saw that more of my West Coast friends were in it: Winona, Walter, Wendy, William and Dweezil whale sharks; and Dolly the Dolphin. Moreover, there was also a ship moored there that seemed to ooze decorum amongst all the bedlam. I should have guessed who was skippering it, but I hadn't seen him for a few months. 'Hello, Grey, my ol' matey, how's it going?' roared a voice from the deck. It was none other than our ol' skipper, Captain Dec O' Rum. I told him I was doing fine, and it was great to see him, before asking where Dai 'on the Seas' was.

Dec said Dai'd sailed in with him the previous day, but had gone into town looking for wine and women, and hadn't returned yet.

It was a magnificent morale booster to see them all again, and a renewed confidence surged through me. After introductions and hugs they helped us cross the river. Although it was a relief that we'd all traversed the water safely, arriving on the other side felt like being on the sharp end of a double-edged sword; because we were now at the foot of Greenslopes, with battalions of Bri's bane protecting the peak.

Notes

The Gap is a Brisbane suburb; as is Indooroopilly.

----

133. ASCENDING GREENSLOPES

Battle of Bri's Bane Epic Trilogy Poem 1

Dead men tell no tales
only the competitive fails
in war there is no sport
to survivors the lesson is taught.

We had not long assembled
before Greenslopes trembled
as balls of fire landed at will
shot from high on Cannon Hill.

Our allies the Woolloongabba
met their Waterloo like Abba
falling in multiple millions
history's cannon fodder minions.

The COG commandos led the counter-attack
up Greenslopes watching each other's back
chinchillas, dogs, humans, wombats and hats
above us flew eagles, dolphins and bats.

Yes, I did say dolphins above us
for a spirit appeared without fuss
and I'm sure it was Kalbarri Barry
riding the sky waves with his family.

Notes

Woolloongabba is a district of Brisbane.
Abba and song: *Waterloo.*

----

134. WILL A HAT-TRICK BE ENOUGH FOR RAIN

Battle of Bri's Bane Epic Trilogy Poem 2

The COG commandos lost legions
fur and skin torn to lesions
rolling back down the slope in heroic death
Chinchillas of Goya drawing their last breath.

I reached the top after an hour of struggle
and saw Bri's bane officers in a huddle
Emily and Brian were flying a pincer attack
Emerald from the front, Baggy from back.

My travel companions and I rushed to help
an arrow glanced Aussie and it gave out a yelp
we continued on through a battlefield royal
the chinchillas and allies staying loyal.

As Brian and Emily approached Bri's bane
the huddle suddenly opened into acid rain
seeming to scent Brian it turned sharply
and flew screeching like a demented harpy.

I shapeshifted into a wolf and raced to Brian
distracting Bri's bane rain as Emily leapt like a lion
Brian jumped for joy as the hats converged
soaking up the acid rain until it was purged.

Notes

The harpy was a winged spirit in Greek mythology.

----

135. THE AFTERMATH

Battle of Bri's Bane Epic Trilogy Poem 3

I lay on the Greenslopes ground
watched by allies all around
Bri's bane was no more
the acid rain cleansed from floor.

'We knew not a wolf you would become,'
said Emily's voice betraying concern,
'for the bane was not only of Brian's
but also of wolves and lions.'

'So wolfsbane is inside you now
but maybe we can work out how
to make you healthy again
I'll try counting to ten.'

Emily counted to eight
my mood improved to third-rate
on nine I sensed the right line
hearing ten I was fine.

I rose to join the others
my sisters and brothers
in arms and hats we had battled
and Bri's Bane together tackled.

136. SEARCHING FOR SURVIVORS AFTER BATTLE OF BRI'S BANE

I rose into a mix of joy and relief; sadness and loss. Many had given their lives on Greenslopes. I was relieved that Angry, Cathy and Elle quickly joined me, and to see they were all in good health. Aussie and Digger soon turned up as well, and were looking swell; Aus said it only received a flesh wound. Then Vombat the Wombat pushed its way through the crowd, with a relieved look on its face. I could see Brian and Emily with the chinchilla survivors, but where were the Collie twins?

Searching for the Collie Twins

I asked the others if they'd seen the Collies. Digger said they'd been fighting heroically the last time it'd seen them, which was near the end of the battle. None of them had seen the Collies at the end of the battle. I started walking down the hill, looking through the bodies, dreading finding the Collies in a bad state.
A cascade of cheers rolled down from the top of the hill. I looked behind me and was filled with relief: the Collie twins were alive and well, and being carried along by a crowd of chinchillas. I rushed up the hill to them, and saw they were all eating buns.
I made my way through the munching mass, and asked the twins where they'd been. Ollie was too busy bun-munching above the bunch to hear; but Colin said that after the fighting finished they noticed a rich bun seam had been exposed by all the disruption, so they'd straightaway started bun-mining to feed the hungry survivors. He handed me a freshly mined rough-cut bun.
I laughed and thanked him, before biting into a bun that tasted just as delicious as those I'd eaten in Bunbury.
As I savoured the taste, and memories of Ozyssey evoked, I thought how Bunbury and Bri's bane were on different sides of Oz, but would be quite close together in a dictionary. I thought there must be a lesson there somewhere, but was too

busy bun-munching to brainwave.

137. SAYING GOODBYE, AND FINDING A NEW PATH

After everybody and everything had their bellies full of buns, Emily and Brian addressed us all; it was nice of them to give us a house.
They also said the locality would now be known as Brisbane, and the region would be called Queensland; in memory of those who had taken part in the battle. They ended by thanking us for freeing Brian from his bane.

The Army Disperses

It was then time to say goodbye to my old friends and comrades, as they departed for home. Captain Dec and Dai were taking Dig, Aus, Vombat and the Collies back to Western Australia, and the cetaceans were swimming that way too. There were of course lots of hugs, and that's all I'm prepared to write here.
After they left, Emily asked us what we were doing next. I had seen the dust sandy path leading inland, but told Emily I didn't know if we were still meant to follow it, now that she and Brian were reunited.
Emily said it looked like the dust sandy path was heading their way... to Emerald.
She invited us along,
and it felt right to go,
for in her I could see a glow;
she hadn't been wrong yet!

138. FOLLOWING THE DUST SANDY PATH TO EMERALD

There was a succulent start to the journey, orienteering through an okay oak forest outside Oakey before devouring a delicious dal dinner in Dalby.

Chinchilla is a Killer... Emotionally

It was Chinchilla next, and I prepared myself for an emotional return. I was not disappointed, with chinchillas lining the streets of Chinchilla as we passed. I saw an old chinchilla rush out of the crowd and hug a COG member. When the COG soldier turned around I was delighted to see the name Cilla Chinchilla on her jacket.

Cilla had survived
and achieved her task.
Now I hoped
she'd have time to bask.

Roma, Orion and Spring

We roamed through Roma, before it turned dark over Orion; which was good timing, as there was a belting night sky there. Then it seemed like it was spring for sure in Springsure, as everything was green. It became evermore evergreen as we neared Emerald.
I asked Emily how everything was so green, and she said these were the Alician Fields. They are a natural wonderland for those who have turned the world upside down to improve it before returning it the right way up; where sparkling spring water irrigates the earth from underground, and the sun always shines above.
I thought nothing could equal the Alician Fields, but Emerald sparkled like the finest precious stone; the town and fields complemented each other like a jewel on silk.
Hats filled the air when Brian and Emily reached Emerald, and our leaders soon joined in with the hatrobatics.

Notes

The Elysian Fields of Greek mythology were a heavenly
paradise for heroic warriors.

----

139. BARRY HUMPHRIES'S GRUMPIES

After it settled down in Emerald I asked Emily if she remembered what MiMo Moby said back in Meekatharra many moons ago; about a Great Dame of Oz at the end of the dust sandy path who could reunite me with Green once again.

Emily said she did remember, and knew exactly what MiMo had meant; she would take us to meet the Dame straight away.

Sir Les Patterson

It wasn't far away; just a couple of blocks to a big mansion in the centre of Emerald. Emily knocked on the door with one of her corks. It wasn't long before a large grumpy man answered it.

He bellowed, 'What do you want?' at us in a rude manner.

'Ah, hello,' said Emily, 'MiMo Moby told this werewolf friend of mine that the Great Dame of Oz should be able to help it. Is she here?'

The man did not seem impressed, but said he'd see if she was around.

The Great Dame of Oz

A woman arrived a few minutes later; she looked like she could be the sister of the man... or even the same person!

'Hello possums,' she said, 'what can I do for you?'

I told her about my conversation with MiMo Moby, and said we were all still quite lost, despite learning a lot on our epic Ozyssey.

She said she'd love to help, and used to do such things, but she was too busy now that she'd become an international giga-star.

Body, Mind and Spirit Work Together Again

I looked at my travel companions; they seemed to share my disappointment. I wondered if my epic ramble had reached an anti-climactic dead-end, and I would never see Green and the Greenygrey world again.

I was about to suggest leaving, when Cathy spoke up in a spirited way, telling the Dame that that was no way to talk to us. Angry seemed to have been thinking about it as well, because he soon added, 'You're not even really the Dame, you were a rude man when you answered the door just now.' Then Elle used her body to great effect by slamming the door shut.

Notes

Sir Les Patterson and Dame Edna Everage are Barry Humphries's comedy characters.

----

140. MOBY TELLS IT AS IT IS, WHICH IS...

We were about to leave, when a porcelain pod came around the corner, and MiMo Moby emerged from it. We were ecstatic, and greeted him with gusto; he seemed equally pleased to see us.

I told him the Dame had been a disappointment, so Angry, Cathy and Elle were uncertain of their future in Oz, and I didn't know if I could return to the Greenygrey world.

Moby Pep Talk

MiMo looked at us all, and then back at Elle, before saying, 'Why, Elle had body issues when she joined you; she had lost all her strength. But she has been using her body with great dexterity throughout the Ozyssey, and now has her confidence back.'

I had to agree. Elle leapt into the air with joy.

'And Angry was letting the *Neighbours'* opinions of his mind get to him; making him feel inadequate. But he has been using fantastic judgement all through the epic adventure, and working well within your travel team.'

Once more, I had to agree. Angry sang a celebratory tune he spontaneously created.

'And Cathy was in low spirits when you met; but freedom, movement, natural space, friendship, being valued and success have helped lift her spirits since joining your epic adventure; and also raised yours at crucial times in this rousing ramble.'

Yet again, I had to agree. Cathy saluted the sun.

'And you, Grey, you have reached your destination, and helped bring the hats of hope home to Emerald. Deep down you know you have the power to return to Green whenever you want. The Greenygrey world is free again; as free as Emerald.'

I thanked MiMo Moby for everything, and we all said hearty farewells before he disappeared around the corner in his porcelain pod. Not long after, Brian arrived from the same direction.

141. SOLO TRAVELLER ONCE AGAIN, LIKE WHEN IT ALL BEGAN

So my epic journey had really ended, and all was well. The Great Dame of Oz left to go on a world tour, so Angry, Elle and Cathy were going to stay in the mansion indefinitely. I'm sure they had bright Emerald futures ahead of them; now they had regained their body, mind and spirit confidence.

Once More unto the Sea

I knew I could return to the Greenygrey world now, but felt there was something else I needed to do. I thought I should visit the Tasman Sea one last time.
So I said cheerio to everybody and everything in Emerald. There were especially long farewells with my three long-term travel companions and my favourite Oz hat couple. Then it was time to go solo once more; returning to my status upon arrival in Oz.

I shapeshifted into a bird of paradise,
and set off once more for the seaside.
I flew with the wind to the east,
for an hour and a half at least,
arriving at the sea over Deception Bay,
I thought there must be another way,
so I headed south and landed next to a jay,
in a place I liked the sound of: Bramble Bay.
I asked the jay, whose name was Jay,
whether it had seen anything untoward astray.
Jay said nothing unusual had happened all day.

Seeing a Sea Commotion

Everything did seem absolutely normal, and I began to wonder if I'd wasted my time making this diversion. But then:
I saw a commotion out at sea
and wondered what it might be.

The commotion was not only there; it was approaching the beach at a phenomenal speed. I asked Jay if it could see it. It said yes, it could.

I wondered what it could be: Was it more acid-rain? Could it be the MoMo East returning from the deep? Or was it Smiggin Holes escaped from its deep hole? Was there one more test I had to put my exhausted bird-brain through? The commotion reached the shallows. I could now make out a head and arms. I thought I recognised who it was... but surely it couldn't be... could it?

It continued swimming to the shallows, and then emerged onto the beach.

142. THE END: OF THE WEREWOLF OF OZ ERA

It was Tazzy! I squawked with joy before flying down to meet him; whereupon I changed back into a more recognisable werewolf form. We greeted before I asked him what he was doing here.
Tazzy said he often swam up this way; after all, it is the Tasman Sea.
I laughed, before exclaiming, 'Of course!' The last riddle of the ramble had been solved... as far as I was concerned. What about you?
I now felt free to return to the Greenygrey world.
Tazzy was continuing north, so I shapeshifted into a dolphin-friendly tuna and swam with him.

We swam side by side
until he dived beneath
to turn around
at top of Barrier Reef;
my original Oz
landmark brief;
we happily said goodbye
finality's welcome relief.

I jumped out of the water and shapeshifted into a wedge-tailed eagle for the long flight back to a long awaited reunion with Green in the Greenygrey world.

Two years in the writing
sometimes flying, mostly hiking
Werewolf of Oz kept moving
experiencing, shapeshifting, grooving.

Thanks for all your company on this epic ramble, and see you back in the Greenygrey world!

http://www.greenygrey.co.uk

Made in the USA
Middletown, DE
28 June 2024

56544145R00129